WINNING WITHOUT WINNING

2nd Edition

Gerry Crowley

authorHOUSE®

AuthorHouse™
1663 Liberty Drive
Bloomington, IN 47403
www.authorhouse.com
Phone: 1-800-839-8640

First published by AuthorHouse 8/4/2010

ISBN: 978-1-4520-4876-5 (e)
ISBN: 978-1-4520-4875-8 (sc)

Library of Congress Control Number: 2010909504

Printed in the United States of America
Bloomington, Indiana

This book is printed on acid-free paper.

CPSIA information can be obtained at www.ICGtesting.com
Printed in the USA
LVOW061844070212

267544LV00001B/33/P

9 781452 048758

- *Winning Without Winning. The title says it all. A concept that 85% of all the people who read Winning Without Winning approve of. And the other 15%? Well you decide. You'll love it. It's all in the book.*

- *You will be affected by Winning Without Winning. It is an excellent reminder of what little league sports should be all about. Anyone who really cares about kids will appreciate this book.*
  Rick Vogel, Minor League Association President.

- *Winning Without Winning is exceptional. It needed to be written 30 years ago. The examples and research make this book interesting and must be read by anyone concerned with our future generations.*
  Robert Huschka, School Board Trustee

- *Crowley calls little league sport of all descriptions a "life-building experience." He shows what good coaching is all about, and what does not qualify as good coaching.*
  Dave Menary, Newspaper Reporter.

- *Crowley and his book are part of a fresh, welcome breeze blowing across the little league sporting scene.*
  Dave Pink, Newspaper Reporter

- *I find the 16th precept (How to Lose) the key factor. Learning from a loss actually improves later performances. The Russians are known to lose non-important games to test the opponents strengths and weaknesses. The end result of a particular game is not important to them.*
  Raymond Stonkus, Canadian Chess Expert.

- *Winning Without Winning is the best book I have ever read concerning youth sports. I bought all of our Middle School Coaches a copy. I cannot begin to tell you how often I have quoted your three questions to ask children after a game. I wish every person who coaches kids at the beginning levels could not only read Winning Without Winning, but truly buy into your concepts. My regret is that I did not have the book when I was coaching kids.*
  Randy Hatfield
  Principal, Borger Intermediate School
  Borger, Texas

ACKNOWLEDGEMENTS

Writing this book was perhaps the most difficult endeavor of my life. But the seemingly endless hours and the emotional roller coaster created a magic for me-real magic, because of the support from so many people who, in one way or another, contributed to the book's evolution.

I name but a few:

Rick Vogel, for without him the book would still be just a thought.

Paul Low, for being my role model.

John Ashby, for creative illustrations that saved a million words.

Terry Whalen, who's input, enhanced the book immeasurably.

Barbara Goodgion, a friend I can always count on.

Derek Crowley, my son, whose tenacious determination to achieve his goals inspires me to achieve my own goals.

Gabriella Currie for her insights, clarity and writing skills.

A NOTE ON THE TEXT

Throughout this book the pronoun "he" has been used to describe both coaches and the children on their teams. This was done for simplicity's sake only, to avoid unwieldy double pronouns. The findings, precepts, anecdotes and suggestions in this book are intended to apply equally to all players and coaches - girls and boys, men and women -involved in all children's activities.

Contents

ACKNOWLEDGEMENTS   vii

A NOTE ON THE TEXT   viii

INTRODUCTION   xi

I: THE WAKE-UP CALL   1

II: YO! WHAT'S UP?   6

III: HEROES, HEROINES, EVERY ONE!   13

IV: GOT COACH?   19

V: I LOVE THESE LITTLE PEOPLE   24

VI: CODE OF BEHAVIOR   31

  Sportsmanship – *1ˢᵗ precept*   *32*
  How to Win / How to Lose – *9ᵗʰ & 16ᵗʰ precepts*   *36*
  How to Compete – *11ᵗʰ precept*   *43*

VII: PARTICIPATION   46

  Setting Goals – *18ᵗʰ precept*   *47*
  Teamwork – *3ʳᵈ precept*   *51*
  Being Fair – *5ᵗʰ precept*   *56*
  Leadership – *10ᵗʰ precept*   *61*

VIII: DEVELOPMENT OF SKILLS   **66**

  Physical Skills – *2nd precept*   *67*
  Learning The Game – *4th precept*   *73*
  Physical Fitness – *12th precept*   *76*

IX: PSYCHOLOGICAL FACTORS   **79**

  Discipline and Self-Control – *7th precept*   *80*
  Motivation – *8th precept*   *84*
  Patience – *13th precept*   *88*
  Resilience – *19th precept*   *92*

X: THE THREE R's   **96**

  Respect – *14th precept*   *97*
  Reliability – *15th precept*   *101*
  Responsibility – *17th precept*   *103*

XI: WHAT IT'S ALL ABOUT   **110**

  Having Fun – *6th precept*   *111*
  Perspective – *20th precept*   *118*

XII: CONCLUSION   **121**

INTRODUCTION

"My hat is in the ring." – *Theodore Roosevelt*

I know it, and you know it: a problem exists in children's sports. Countless interpretations abound, but when all is said and done, there is one central problem.

That problem is a focus on *winning* at all costs, and this problem does not start with the children.

As a youngster I participated in sports. Like all children, I experienced some good times and times I'd rather forget. I grew up, got married, and had children of my own. Then, as many people do, I continued to participate in kid's sports-this time as a coach. I love sports, I love children and I love to coach. So it only made sense that I'd love coaching kids.

After several years of coaching, the sports organization in which I participated invited me to join their executive board. As a member of the governing body, I went to increasingly more games and tournaments at a variety of age levels, from those played by four-year-olds just learning rudimentary physical skills to those featuring the league's adolescent all-stars. At this point I realized my personal involvement in sports had progressed full-circle. I went from being a shy hesitant onlooker child to an enthusiastic participant, then to a deeply motivated coach, and then to an altruistically inspired board member, official and administrator, and then back to being a hesitant onlooker. But this time my hesitation was for a different reason.

Something was awry. Violence broke out at games and officials, parents, and even children were verbally abused during games. Some people even had to be ejected. Very often children dejectedly exited the playing area after games. The atmosphere was frequently tense, nervous, and unhappy.

Who was unhappy…The children…The adults? *Both* groups were unhappy!

Why were both children and adults unhappy? The perceived needs of both groups were not being met. The kids simply wanted to have fun-which is why they were there in the first place. But the adults were keen on a different objective-winning.

Children play sports to have fun. They have a need for exercise, fellowship, and new-skill learning. Parents and coaches sometimes confuse their longing to see the children succeed with a desire to win at all cost. A major problem occurs when adults fail to recognize the needs of the children or put their own superficial needs ahead of the legitimate needs of the children. The problem is magnified when they judge success by the scoreboard.

This was the problem that needed to be explored. In order to gather as much data as I could, I attended hundreds of games in various sports for both girls and boys. What was I hoping to find? I wasn't sure, but I knew there had to be a common element.

I took notes as I spoke with children, coaches, parents and other league organizers. I asked for input and eventually received more than 4000 responses from those involved at different levels of children's sports. The most moving were letters from adults who shared their own early sports experiences. They recounted childhood incidents that occurred during their years in Babe Ruth leagues, youth hockey, peewee football, pigtail softball, recreation league soccer, "junior-pro" basketball, and other children's sports programs. Their reminiscence revealed vivid memories of events that they claimed had affected their adult lives.

Some memories were positive. But far too many memories were negative. That indicated that there was a problem deep-rooted in children's sports.

I wanted to address this problem. It was my hope then, and it is still my hope today, that by creating an awareness of what children are learning in organized sports, and the unintended detrimental effects thereof, we can redefine the philosophy of youth sports to recapture the healthy values inherent to children's sports.

This book is about children. Our children today depend on us-the adults-for their every need, but tomorrow they will be the adults making their own decisions. The actions they take tomorrow depend directly on the actions we take today.

Children need to play and to have fun. Studies have shown that they learn more and perform better when they enjoy what they are doing. Just as toddlers learn as they explore their environment, older children also learn during play. If the play is fun, participation will increase and the opportunity for advanced learning likewise is enhanced.

Having fun nurtures inner strength. A child cannot help but smile.

Among the important lessons that our children can learn from organized sports is the ability to feel good about their own personal accomplishments and their contributions to the team as a whole. This creates a winning attitude that is a foundation to positive self-esteem. As parents and coaches, it is our job to see that our children's needs are met. Just as important as food and shelter is the need for positive self worth. We must be aware of the opportunities we have to instill a sense of winning in our children during their play. To do this, it is critical that we are mindful of what winning really is and that we understand that it is our responsibility to make all children feel like winners-for the sake of the children. And are they not those for whom we toil?

Creating a winning attitude is not magic. It's attitude. And it works!

I: THE WAKE-UP CALL

"If you can keep your head when all about you are losing theirs . . . then you will be a man, my son." –
Rudyard Kipling

I had a theory, albeit an untested one, and I was excited about gathering support for it. Each year at the children's year-end baseball tournament there were fights and ejections. One year, during the six-year-olds' tournament, a parent became so abusive he had to be removed from the field by police. Can you imagine the looks on the faces of the players to see an adult placed in a police cruiser and taken away? How must his child have felt? I was determined that this should never happen again.

To that end I held a seminar focusing on a new perspective-awareness. Twenty-eight adults attended, most of them coaches. The results were surprisingly predictable. How can something be both surprising and predictable? The outcome was a surprising reminder that all too often the obvious objectives of youth sports were not being achieved.

I began by welcoming everyone to a new concept-winning without winning. I explained that my goal was to make coaches aware of what was required of them when they decided to coach children.

I started by asking, "What are a coach's duties?"

A discussion followed about being on time, having the equipment there, etc. Then I asked a different kind of question: "What should coaches be teaching children?" The lively dialogue that resulted suggested I had hit a nerve.

So, we brainstormed-the same kind of brainstorming used in business and industry. Each participant wrote down a list of five things coaches should teach kids. (We'll discuss these in detail later in this book.) How often are you driving in the car or just drifting off to sleep and something really important pops into your mind? You think you'll remember it later, or in the morning, but most often it simply vanishes from your thoughts-unless you write it down. It is certainly too easy to forget unless you see it in black and white. Furthermore, an idea is futile unless it's implemented and writing ideas down is the first step to ultimately achieving goals. Coaches are naturally creative and insightful. Their ideas contribute to the success of their leagues and the enjoyment of the players. It only made sense that the coaches themselves could shed light on what is best for their players. The collective thoughts of the coaches were necessary to identify those issues.

So each individual picked up his or her pencil and began. The only stipulation was that they had to begin with the sentence "I believe coaches should be teaching kids..." and then continue with the list. During our discussion, and after, the feedback was fantastic. In fact, the next day I had one coach call to tell me that because of that seminar, she realized that the principles that coaches should teach young athletes are the same principles that parents should teach their children. She had had an ongoing family dispute with her teenage daughter whereas she and her daughter had not spoken to each other in two weeks. She applied the brainstorming principle to her family situation by asking herself what she should be teaching her child. She took the next step by implementing the changes required to remedy the conflict, and the results were successful. She and her daughter were, once again, on good terms.

This coach, as well as her peers, had become students themselves. They had learned new concepts at the seminar and practiced what they learned on the ball fields. Each game showed improved attitudes and by that year's final tournament a new mind-set had emerged. Most coaches remembered that the children were there to improve personal skills and, above all, to have fun.

During one particularly tense tournament game, an umpire was out of position and made an indisputably incorrect call. The wronged team was upset and trouble seemed imminent. Then the unexpected happened. The coach called his infield together at the pitcher's mound and in a loud voice proclaimed, "Boys, we're here to have fun. Forget the call." Forget the call? We were all dumbstruck. Mouths dropped and eyes blinked in disbelief. A look of astonishment appeared on the faces of the kids. A bad call by an umpire didn't matter?

What a pleasant change from angry words, elevated stress levels, teary eyes, hurt feelings and damaged egos. The calm was the result of simple words that demonstrated a simple philosophy, spoken by a man who, days earlier, would have lost his temper. The seminar had given this coach the opportunity to be made aware that his past outbursts were unsuccessful in getting umpires to reverse calls, as well as also ineffective in teaching children. He not only eliminated his inappropriate behavior, he replaced it with positive, constructive advice.

Was it magic? Was it a miracle? Whatever you call it, this simple philosophy needed a broader audience. So, after countless meetings, endless discussions, and an unfaltering belief, *Winning without Winning* was created.

FOR PARENTS AND COACHES

Make your own list of what you think coaches should be teaching children. As you work through this book, compare and consider what you have written with what is presented in these pages. Compare notes with colleagues and other parents. Expand and amend your list to suit your own situation and to include practical examples that relate directly to your own organization. Coaches, hold a pre-season meeting with parents for the combined purposes of gathering required permission forms, distributing schedules, and brainstorming to set both individual and joint goals for the season. The chances for a successful season will increase if both the coaching staff and the parents have the same goals and are teaching the children the same standards.

II: YO! WHAT'S UP?

"In youth we learn; in age we understand." – Marie Ebner-Eschenbach

Thus is a problem in youth sports. Ever increasing rumblings from coaches, spectators, game officials and participants themselves indicate the problem's magnitude. You only have to check your local newspaper for letters to the editor to confirm this. Something is wrong, and it permeates every facet of youth sports, regardless of activity, gender or age.

The heading read "Baseball Season Taught Poor Lessons for Life" when the following letter to the editor appeared in a local newspaper.

> *My 15-year-old son has been playing baseball and hockey since he was six, yet I have never been so discouraged as during this past poorly organized season. Nor have I seen such a display of outbursts and bad temper.*
>
> *To begin, my pre-registration check was mailed in December and cashed in January. Then we waited.*
>
> *In the past, ball practices have normally begun at the end of April or beginning of May. This year, my son waited for weeks for a call from a coach to say when practices would begin, when his first game would be played or what team he would play on.*
>
> *At the end of May, after several messages I left on an answering machine, I was informed that, sorry, they didn't have coaches! Should sports organizations that have cashed one's check months in advance not have the courtesy to at least inform players of the situation about coaches and other arrangements.*

When finally we were on a team they then informed us that there would be no practices-there were no ball diamonds available.

When the season finally got under way, arguments broke out at several of the games. Several others were rained out. Those were to be rescheduled, yet at the last game of the season we were informed that the rained-out games were not going to be played.

And let me tell you about that last game. Before it began, an umpire, who was not officiating that day, got into an argument with the coaches. Then he left, and the game began. About halfway through the game another argument broke out, this time between the two game umpires and the coaches. There were tense moments. Words were exchanged and I wondered if they were going to come to blows! Finally, the umpire told the children to go home-the game was over. Those children begged him. They pleaded, 'It's our last game. Please, let us play.' But the game was over.

Youth sports aren't cheap. I paid for my son to play ball for a full season. I feel he has been cheated and should be reimbursed for the failure to reschedule certain games.

What has this season taught our children? 'It's okay, we have your money. Nothing you can do about it.' It has taught them to swear, argue, raise their tempers and come close to fistfights. Whatever happened to good sportsmanship and going out to have a good time?

Three strikes-you're out. I feel that the three strikes came before the season even started.

What did happen to good sportsmanship and going out to have a good time? I'm sure you feel this parent's frustration as personally as I do. Her complaints are valid-her son learned negative values from his experience with youth sports that season. It is beyond sad that those boys wanted so desperately just to play ball and instead, through circumstances that had nothing to do with them, their last game of the season was cancelled.

Children are full of enthusiasm and optimism. Life, to them, is full of possibilities. The memory of a caught fly-ball, played on a loop again and again in their minds, will last forever. This is the stuff dreams are made of. Yet we tamper with those dreams by abusing the positions of authority we are in. We, the parents and coaches, have the power to build or to destroy, and that is an awesome responsibility.

As with every story, there are two sides, so in the interests of fair play I have included the umpire's response to that parent's letter, which also appeared in the letters to the editor section some days later.

I would like to come to an understanding with 'Pat' about her letter entitled, 'Baseball Season Taught Poor Lessons for Life'.

Considering how many leagues there are in this area, baseball diamonds are in short supply. League directors won't know how many diamonds they are going to get until the city tells them. Coaches are volunteers who offer their time. They, too, are in limited supply.

'Pat's' money covers the cost of maintaining the diamonds, such as putting the lines down, and paying umpiring fees so she can have umpires at the games.

> *Being an umpire in one hundred or so games this year,*
> *I am judge, jury and executioner out on the playing*
> *field. An umpire pays for his own equipment and is*
> *out there as much to serve the children playing baseball*
> *as are the coaches, but paid to know the rules. Umpires*
> *don't like ejections or forfeits either, for the same reason*
> *'Pat' cited about what they teach children. Umpires*
> *are human. We make mistakes, but that's life. Some*
> *of the rules call for ejection and/or game forfeiture*
> *as a way of calming down a situation such as the one*
> *cited by 'Pat'. There is nothing else an umpire can do,*
> *according to the rulebook.*
>
> *Why doesn't 'Pat' become a coach? Failing that,*
> *she could become an umpire. She would have a greater*
> *appreciation for all that goes on behind the scenes*
> *rather than complaining about it.*

Coaches are volunteers-true. Umpires serve children for much the same reason as do coaches-true. Umpires make mistakes-true. Umpires are human-true. Yet, in all of this some very important details have been overlooked. What lessons are the children learning? Who controls what the children learn? When does the fun begin?

In his response the umpire states that game ejection and game forfeiture are necessary to calm certain situations down. That begs the questions of why we create situations that escalate through anger, necessitating an umpire's drastic interventions. It matters very little who is right and who is wrong. Do we want to teach our children that ranting and raving is the way to handle anger?

Children are constantly learning. The younger they are the more impressionable they are. It is our job to present children with positive learning experiences, not negative ones. The example that we set is the lead children will follow.

Consider this scenario.

A mother and her son are in an elevator. Suddenly, the lights go out and the elevator shudders to a halt. The child is about to panic and tears well up in his eyes. He calls to his mother who has remained calm and reassures him that everything is all right. Help is on the way. She gives him a hug and his world is safe once again. He trusts her and follows her lead until the situation is resolved. This lesson will be stored in the child's memory to become a part of his coping mechanism. However, had she behaved irrationally-screaming and crying in terror-you can bet that that too would have been burned into the child's memory, giving him quite a different set of coping skills for life. We often take our own actions for granted, not realizing that they have a direct impact on a child's state of mind, now and for the future.

The same lesson applies to the relationship between a coach and his team. If the coach is out to win at all costs, his team will believe that they, too, must win at all costs. If the coach gets angry and throws equipment, his team will learn that when they get angry they, too, can throw equipment. It is paramount in life for each one of us to learn to deal constructively with our anger, because anger leads to…. I'll let you finish the sentence.

If the coach complains and yells at the officials, then his team will also feel they can complain and yell at the officials. A child's developing sense of logic might tell him that if it's okay to yell at an official, then it must also be okay to yell at his teacher, his parents, and others in his life.

Are you getting the picture? The consequences of those examples are negative lessons learned for life. These children then carry these lessons into other aspects of their lives and on into adulthood. The flip-side is true as well, so coaches and parents need to always be aware that this transference of learning also occurs when children encounter positive attitudes through sports. Positive experiences create and instill positive values about the game of life. A coach's obsession to win at all costs could impair the developing psyche of a child, whereas a coach's healthy perspective about winning could lead to favorable development.

FOR PARENTS AND COACHES

Briefly jot down experiences that you had as children in recreational sports that affected you or others negatively. Consider how adults could have turned those negative events into neutral, non-eventful occurrences or even positive memories. Then write down recent experiences in the lives of your children and the children you coach that may have a negative impact. Consider ways in which these events could have been handled differently and ways you can address those issues now, before they have a negative long-term impact.

III: HEROES, HEROINES, EVERY ONE!

"If Hero mean 'sincere man,' why may not every one of us be a Hero? - Carlyle

In all my research, never once did I see it written that a hero is the winner of a game. The root of the word "hero" is Greek in origin and it means, simply, *protector.* Or, as the dictionary tells us, a hero is someone who is admired for his brave and noble deeds. Every day there are noble deeds performed by ordinary people like you and me. We are all heroes who strive to be kind and helpful in our everyday lives. So being a hero doesn't necessarily mean hitting a home run, scoring the winning goal, or dunking from the free-throw stripe. Doing something right for the team makes you just as much a hero. Trying, against all odds, makes you a hero.

Jesse was a pretty typical eleven-year-old boy who loved baseball and played little league every year. He was never among the best players on the team. During one particular game, Jesse was standing in right field waiting anxiously for the next pitch. Smack! A line-drive to right field. Jesse held his breath and charged the ball, hoping to make a shoestring catch to end the inning. The ball hit the ground just inches from his outstretched glove. Jesse stretched some more and the ball short-hopped right into his glove. The runner on first base, by this time, was rounding second base on his way to third. Instinct took over and Jesse fired the ball to third base. The bullet was waist high and in time. We all expected an out, but the third baseman dropped the ball. The runner was safe but Jesse didn't care. He had never thrown the ball so fast and so true in his life and this was his moment of glory. Spectators cheered and applauded. They knew they had seen something that rarely happens for a player of Jesse's caliber.

Jesse felt like a hero.

An out later the inning was up and the team ran back to the dugout. Everyone was cheering Jesse's effort again and he grinned from ear to ear. He felt like Derek Jeter. Jesse felt like a hero! If only the story ended there.

Unfortunately, Jesse's play was not part of the team repertoire. He was supposed to have used the cutoff man.

"That's not what we practiced!" the coach yelled.

And then, in an overbearing manner, he chastised Jesse, spewing his venom on his unsuspecting victim whose greatest effort now was trying to hold back the tears.

What could have been-should have been-a memory of a lifetime will now be remembered as a moment of incredible humiliation for poor Jesse. True, the throw should have been to the cutoff man and the next time in that situation, he may very well throw to the cutoff man. Lesson learned. But can you say the coach was correct with how he handled the situation? Was the fear, intimidation, and humiliation worth the lesson learned? Could his good throw have been praised, followed by a gentle reminder of what they had practiced? Will Jesse feel pressure or pleasure in executing new skills the next time? Coaches are in a powerful position to teach skills and how they deliver their lessons can either build or damage the self-esteem of a child.

Was Jesse was a hero that day when he thought he had achieved a personal best? Everybody thought it except for one dangerous coach who thought the lesson learned was more important than understanding that particular child's "personal best".

I've received letters about various experiences in youth sports from all over the world. Some expressed positive memories while others still felt the discomfort of a hurtful experience. Many of the letters had one thing in common. The writer could seldom remember the outcome of the game! Within most games there are moments of triumph that will be remembered by someone forever. Your coaching will create memories. What kind of memories will your coaching create?

**Yup! My best catch ever! Hmm...
I wonder if we won that game?**

The outcome of the game is insignificant compared to what a child can really learn from your coaching. Your conduct can directly influence a child's attitude, one that he could carry with him the rest of his life. Coaches have the ability to make heroes. The sense of accomplishment a child feels when he is a "hero" is a building block in his life. This attitude has the potential to pervade every decision he makes, perhaps even as to how he will treat his own children. You have that power. It's an awesome responsibility.

Gerry Crowley

FOR PARENTS AND COACHES

Consider whether your efforts are focused only on *winning* every game, and what effect this aim is having on the children involved. Try to pick out at least one "hero" each game. Recognize and praise his efforts and not his ability.

IV: GOT COACH?

"He is wise who can instruct us and assist us in the business of daily virtuous living." - Carlyle

Many adults wind up as coaches by default. This happened during my son's first year of soccer. Like a tail with no dog, fifteen eager children turned up for the first practice of the year, only to be told by members of the recreation department that unless a parent volunteered to coach, there would be no team this year. Try to explain that to a seven-year-old. Yet this happens all too often.

If you've picked up this book because you've decided to volunteer as a coach, bravo! Without people like you there would be scores of bored, unmotivated children. Coaching is a very generous gesture and, despite some issues, sports play an important role in the development of children. Remember, though, that coaching is a responsibility that goes far beyond the physical skills of a child. Are you up for it?

Let's examine the duties and responsibilities that go along with the position. Coaching positions don't come with job descriptions and except for select teams, the organizations generally do little to assist coaches' efforts. So, the X's and O's of what you'll teach and how you'll teach are largely your decisions.

Where do you start? First, ask yourself, "What should I be teaching the children?" Take a few moments to consider the answers and write your thoughts down. Having these ideas on paper, in your own handwriting, is the first step to developing a meaningful agenda. Coaches have to create their own objectives in furtherance of their mission. From your initial notes, practice sessions can be planned and game strategies formulated. Much like businesses that allow their values and vision to guide them through a well-defined strategic plan, coaches too have to map out their direction. Thoughtful pre-season planning and a written mission statement that defines your objectives will keep you on track during the season. Sure, you might see that your team needs more practice time in areas that you did not foresee, but your overall mission does not have to change because of tactical adjustments. Once well-defined goals are established, the "how to teach" will not be overshadowed by the "what to teach".

As you develop your objectives, it's important to remember that children develop differently. Some have physical talents that may very well determine their path in life. But for the vast majority of children, attitude will be what determines not only where they go in life, but also how they handle life's ups and downs. It is important to be cognizant of your role in the development of your children's attitudes.

The dictionary defines a coach as someone who trains athletes, and it defines an athlete as someone who is strong, vigorous and muscular. The trouble is that not all children are athletes. Children are unfinished business-works-in-progress that need nurturing and guidance. A coach must be a teacher, a leader and a role model.

There has been much said in the media today about the importance of role models. Professional athletes like Drew Brees, Kevin Durant, LeBron James, Sidney Crosby, Derek Jeter, Dustin Pedroia, Phil Mickelson, etc., recognize the responsibility they carry because they are idolized by young boys and girls. Their actions are scrutinized because that is what children do. They mimic without knowing that's what they're doing. There is none so observant of detail as a child!

As a coach in kid's sports, your influence on these impressionable innocents is even more important, because you are *real*. You are a part of their lives in a tangible way and your contact with them has direct cause and effect. Unfortunately, some coaches are more concerned with their own reputations than with the real matter of developing growth experiences through participation in sports.

There are approximately five million active coaches across the country, each with about thirteen children on a team. You do the math. It means that there are an astronomical number of lessons being passed on each year, and many of these stymie self-esteem and confidence.

Unfortunately, few coaches come equipped with much more than the basic knowledge of the game they are coaching. They put too much emphasis on winning. So, what should you be teaching the children? Read on.

FOR PARENTS AND COACHES

What other issues need to be addressed for you to prepare your mission? Should it make a difference what the talent level of your team is? Should you emphasize learning and having fun only in the years when your talent is weak? Are you tempted to emphasize winning more when you see that you do have a shot at the league title?

Ask yourself whether coaches and parents in your sports organization allow their own needs or egos to supersede the needs of the children. Can you tell what coaches' and parents' personal objectives are by how coaches coach and by what parents say? The pre-season meeting would be a good time to share your objectives with the parents, so that they would better understand your coaching style throughout the season.

V: I LOVE THESE LITTLE PEOPLE

"For titles do not reflect honor on men, but rather men on their titles." – Machiavelli

In my quest to answer the question, "What should coaches be teaching the children?" it was possible to arrive at a consensus of lessons, or precepts, that coaches should pass on to the children. Parents, coaches, officials, and recreation department personnel were asked to provide a list of what they believed children should be learning. About 2,500 lists were gathered. Responses came from stakeholders at youth sign-ups, sports seminars, schools, and via the Internet, representing a cross-section of athletic disciplines and therefore a reasonable representation of opinion. The lists were analyzed. In order of prevalence, the top twenty responses are as follows:

Sportsmanship
Physical Skill
Teamwork
Learning the Game
Being Fair
Having Fun
Discipline and Self-control
Motivation
How to Win
Leadership
How to Compete
Physical Fitness
Patience
Respect
Reliability
How to Lose
Responsibility

Setting Goals
Resilience
Perspective

Experts recognize the impact of sports on a developing character. Lessons learned from athletics can have life-long effects.

There is an indisputable link between participation in sports and building positive self-esteem, provided, of course, that the participation is meaningful. Without self-esteem, a child can never properly develop strength of character. Child psychologists have determined that there are also many indirect benefits, such as a sense of belonging that comes from joining with team members for a common goal and a feeling of satisfaction knowing that you are important to your team and that they like you. The American sports psychologist, Dr. Eric Margenau, summed it up beautifully when he wrote: *"For society in general, sports creates a reason for people to come together, for sharing a communality of experience, for developing self-esteem, and for enriching the inner life through fantasy."*

In light of the opinions of experts recognizing the genuine value of sports for developing children, ask yourself once more, "What should I be teaching the children?"

The lessons to be taught to young athletes are quite different from objectives of professional sports. Aside from both playing the same game, the business of professional sports has very little in common with youth organizations. As you are developing your objectives from your list or the precepts provided, keep in mind that it is you who is the *true* coach, whereas professional coaches are facilitators working in a highly competitive business. The differences in the objectives of children's sports and professional sports should be obvious. Youth lessons are a long way from the tainted "win at all costs" philosophy that nevertheless so many children's coaches embrace.

While the teaching philosophies should be different between youth sports and professional sports children will naturally identify with, and admire, professional athletes. Too often children are exposed to inappropriate adult issues of professional athletes. However, some pros behave in ways we may want our children to emulate. When parents and coaches learn of pros behaving in positive ways, they should make a mental note of the incident and use the example at a time when it benefits the children. For example, Greg Norman lost the 1996 Masters after he blew a six-shot lead. One sports reporter called it "One of the biggest chokes." But Norman came out a hero by gracefully accepting the defeat as one of life's unexpected trials. "It's not the end of the world," he said. "I'll get up tomorrow morning still breathing, I hope." An editorial in the *New York Times* empathized: "Anyone who has ever flubbed a job interview, gone blank in the middle of delivering a speech, or double-faulted to lose a set, can identify with Greg Norman." Can you foresee a time when retelling that story would benefit your children?

Similarly, in 1987, the incomparable Boris Becker, the youngest Wimbledon winner at the time, lost to a young Australian. Reporters clambered to record Becker's public suffering.

"Is this your most disappointing defeat ever?" cried one reporter.

"No, I've lost tougher matches. Look, I tried my best and I lost. I'm human. I cannot play good every day. But there was no war, no one was killed. It was just a tennis match."

You simply cannot ascribe the tenets of professional sports to recreation leagues. It would be a little like comparing the responsibilities of the chief executive officer of Coca-Cola to those of a child and her lemonade stand. Every parent knows that little Erica isn't going to get rich from selling lemonade to customers on the curb, but she's learning valuable life lessons. Try telling the CEO of Coca-Cola it isn't important if he shows a profit this year as long as he is honest and diligent in his work. Wouldn't that be an interesting conversation to overhear?

The importance of most decisions depends entirely on perspective.

The same understanding must be applied to sports. By their very definition professional sports are about money and profit, and only indirectly about athletics and fun. Vince Lombardi, coach of the Super Bowl winning Green Bay Packers once said, "Winning isn't everything, it's the only thing." He can be forgiven for his delusion by bearing in mind that the stakes are high in the NFL. A professional coach has legitimate concerns about his reputation for winning because his future is largely measured by the Win / Loss column. Coaches at that level are certainly not there to teach professional athletes important lessons about life values. The chasm between coaching pros and coaching children is wide and deep!

The following chapters examine the precepts that were identified as lessons that children ought to learn through youth sports.

But first, let me introduce you to Coach Eddie. He is not fictional-he is as real as you and me. He has coached children's teams in a variety of sports for over twenty years. But don't look to Coach Eddie as our model coach. In fact, he is quite the opposite, and stands as an example of part of what is wrong within youth sports. Coach Eddie applies the rules of professional sports to little league, believing that you must win at all costs. Applying the logic of Vince Lombardi to recreation department games, he thinks winning is the "only thing". But don't judge him too harshly, lest you recognize him in the mirror. Coach Eddie is doing what he sincerely believes is right. Unfortunately, he lacks perspective awareness.

FOR COACHES AND PARENTS

Compare your list of what you think coaches should be teaching with the list provided in the above chapter. Add new items that you find appropriate from this list to your list. As you go through this book, note which precepts are already being taught well by your sports organization. Mark the areas where questions are raised and problems exist. This will create a list of areas that need improvement. Each precept in the next six chapters is followed by questions and suggestions to aid in your assessment of how well you and your organization are doing in these important areas.

VI: CODE OF BEHAVIOR

O f the twenty precepts identified as goals to teach in youth sports, four directly relate to the code of behavior. This chapter examines those four precepts, which are as follows:

Sportsmanship

How to Win

How to Lose

How to Compete

Sportsmanship – *1st precept*

"Young men soon give and soon forget affronts."
– Addison

When the votes were tallied, sportsmanship was clearly the number one response from coaches and parents when asked what they wanted their children to learn through youth sports leagues. What exactly is sportsmanship? Why do most people feel this is what coaches should be teaching children? Just how important is it?

At the outset, it is important for coaches to realize that new players will not automatically know the unwritten rules of sportsmanship. Even well mannered children who are always polite may not know proper sports etiquette. Young players will not know the proper things to say to the opposing players after a game. They will not know what they should or should not do during time-outs when other players are hurt. They will follow your lead for their first lessons on sportsmanship. Teaching sportsmanship is a perfect opportunity for your children to understand the meaning of *empathy*.

The dictionary defines sportsmanship as fair-mindedness. Our grandmothers would define it better by saying sportsmanship is synonymous with the Golden Rule.

You lost - be a good sport about it.
You won - be a good sport about it.

The quality of behavior of individuals in both victory and defeat is what sportsmanship is all about. In any sport, as in life, mistakes are inevitable. To accept this is to understand that a person's value is not determined by his accomplishments on the playing field. To the truly sportsmanlike individual, mistakes are learning experiences. Properly handled, this message will be passed along to the children.

Make mistakes a learning experience.

In effect, when you create an environment of sportsmanship, you are giving your charges a proper perspective awareness. They will know how to win well, to lose well, and to remember, above all, that it is a game, a diversion, a way to have fun!

FOR PARENTS AND COACHES: SPORTSMANSHIP

Do you believe sportsmanship is being promoted in your sports organization? Consider how parents, coaches, and children react to mistakes, errors, game losses and game wins. Do children mock each other after games? Is humiliation tolerated?

How to Win / How to Lose – *9th & 16th precepts*

"It is the contest that delights us, and not the victory."
- Pascal

"There are some defeats more triumphant than victories." - Montaigne

Instruction should include teaching the youngsters to be good winners as well as good losers. Before their first game, players should be reminded that winning is not something to gloat over. Kids are naturally shortsighted and they will need to be told that although they won this time, it is probable that they will lose at some point. Knowing and understanding this will help them win graciously. Being a gracious winner is part of the positive attitude that needs to be passed on to the kids on your team.

The importance you place on winning will largely determine the children's attitudes about winning. Many t-ball coaches have to tell their team after the game whether they won or lost. Yet others place so much emphasis on winning that their teams experience tension the entire game.

Coach Eddie certainly knows how to win. He uses his best players as much as the rules allow, while less-skilled children play only the required minimum. As will any coach out to win at all costs, he figured out a way to abide by rules and still play the game his way. He would put weaker players in for only *one pitch* during two consecutive innings to satisfy the "must play two innings" rule. With tears welling they would ask to be put back in the game, only to be told, "go home and don't come back until you grow up!" Some never did come back. They probably decided that the being on a winning team wasn't enough-they wanted to play, to feel part of the team. Coach Eddie won the championship that year.

When normal, healthy, developing children are put in a situation where the only absolute is to win, they become anxious, and an anxious child cannot function or develop properly. Given the choice, most children will walk away from a situation that makes them feel bad about themselves. Contrary to what some believe, toughing it out with a verbally abusive coach will not build character. It can lead to loss of sleep or appetite, or the child might develop physical ailments brought on by stress. We acknowledge the evils of stress in adulthood: irritability, high blood pressure, risk of stroke or heart attack, or general depression. It is no less damaging to a child, and maybe even more so. According to Dr. Eric Margenau, *"When the emphasis is placed solely on winning or advancing, most of the healthy aspects of athletics are lost."*

Winning is not hard to do-winning graciously is. First, it is important to insist that no one belittle any member of the opposing team. Then you should remind your team that a win today is nice, but there are no guarantees for the next time.

Naturally, every parent wants his or her child to be a winner, but whether or not this is a good thing depends on your definition of winning. The dictionary gives us a variety to choose from:

- To be victorious in a battle, game or race.
- To obtain or achieve as the result of a battle or contest or bet.
- To obtain as a result of effort or perseverance.
- To gain the favor or support of.
- To succeed after a struggle in reaching a certain state or place.

Convince the children that they can be winners without victorious games. The very fact that they are there makes them a winner. As a parent, a teacher, a coach, it is your responsibility to help your child develop a healthy perspective on winning. Doing so may require you to redefine what "winning" means to you personally.

Even harder than teaching a child how to be a good winner is the task of teaching him how to be a good loser. Usually it is the most competitive player who has the hardest time accepting defeat. Characteristics that typically accompany a competitive personality are usually desirable traits, such as tenaciousness, so it can be challenging to teach a child to keep his tenacious, hard-working, competitive attitude, but not to worry about losing.

You'll want the children to realize that you are aware of their desire to win. In fact, you'll want them to know that you'd like for them to win as well, but that you will still consider the game a victory if they lose as long as they achieve other successes during the contest. Kids need to learn that accepting a loss is equally important as celebrating a win. Losing should simply be looked upon as a passing experience in life – one that certainly has nothing to do with self-worth.

Channel that competitive energy positively.

How to lose graciously is one of life's lessons that must have eluded Coach Eddie. One game his team was winning by one run. When David, his center fielder, dropped a fly ball it resulted in a tie game. Coach Eddie went ballistic the moment the ball hit the ground, almost as though he expected David to drop the ball. He screamed for the fielder to get his butt on the bench, while a teammate ran out to take David's place. David, just a boy, cowered on the bench while Coach Eddie convinced him of his worthlessness! Coach Eddie humiliated David in front of his teammates and his parents who were sitting in the stands. What must have been going through that child's mind as he sat trembling on the bench? He dropped a

Gerry Crowley

ball! Did that really warrant malevolence? Possibly Coach
Eddie believed he was teaching David a lesson by scolding
him; but more likely, Coach Eddie was just a sore loser
who took out his frustrations on his players. Coach Eddie
was teaching all the wrong lessons about losing.

"Do you know how to lose?" This is a question every
little league coach should ask of himself. I queried a
number of coaches and was taken aback by some of the
scorn tossed at me. I fielded replies such as:

- *"Losing is not an option."*
- *"Don't say that word in front of the kids!"*
- *"If we lost, it's because we didn't try hard enough."*
- *"How to lose? Sure, you lose because you play lousy."*
- *"You're not supposed to know how to lose because you don't ever want to get used to losing."*
- *"You don't have to know how to lose, it just happens and you feel lousy about it."*

These erroneous, albeit well-meant, comments give
us insight into an attitude that is being passed on to
thousands of children everyday. Although an adult may
know how to put such acrimony into perspective, a child
certainly does not. A child learns to equate losing with
not being good enough.

If we never learn how to lose with dignity, life will
hold many bitter memories for us indeed. Children look
to adults for direction and leadership. They often believe
their coaches know more about the game than their

parents do, and if coach says that losing is for losers, what is a child to think?

There is nothing wrong with losing, so long as they take a lesson from each loss. What they learn may not necessarily make them winners the next time, but it will teach them more about themselves, and it will move them in a positive direction. Therefore, learning how to lose is just as important as learning how to win, yet so little is understood about the philosophy of losing. It should not be something that you simply tolerate between wins. Losing is not about being less worthy. Children need to believe that losing is a learning experience. We could teach children that losing is a gauge of sorts, a measure for improvement. We should encourage them to do their best and to learn from mistakes. When children involved in any sport or game are having fun while learning, there is no such thing as losing!

As children grow older, winning becomes more important to them. The competitive spirit stirs and grows. It is the job of both parents and coaches to channel that competitive energy positively.

Gerry Crowley

FOR PARENTS AND COACHES: HOW TO WIN/HOW TO LOSE

What is your definition of winning? Are children being taught to win graciously, appreciating their opponents' efforts? Are they being taught to take defeat in stride, to learn from their mistakes? Are they rewarded for actual effort, rather than punished for "losing"?

How to Compete – *11ᵗʰ precept*

"None but yourself who are your greatest foe." - Longfellow

Game time is much more than matching one team's attained skills against an opponent's to produce a winning side. Teach children that "how to compete" begins before the kids arrive at the game and continues after the game is over. Encourage the kids to start thinking about the game before they arrive and to think about implementing the skills they have been practicing. After the game encourage the kids to think about their own personal performance and how they could have improved. Studies have indicated that thinking about the game before it begins enhances performance. Pre-game meditation and visualization are not uncommon among higher level athletes. Mental preparation for a game is similar to studying for an upcoming test in school. It is effective and should be encouraged because it will extend to other areas of the child's life. Game time is also an opportunity to teach children the gestures of accepting defeat and winning graciously. The handshake and congratulatory "good game" at the end of each match consoles the losing side while at the same time recognizes the victors-simple exercises but amazing ways to teach kids the unwritten rules of how to compete.

When the children compete they should be testing their skills in friendly rivalry. That's what amateur competition is all about. It is meant to be fun, exciting and leave the children with fond memories. Attempts to coach using professional-level techniques and aggression are not only inappropriate, but can be damaging to youth league athletes.

Consider two scenarios. The owner of a major league franchise confronts his general manager about their fifth straight loss. The GM explains, "It's not whether you win or lose, it's how you play the game." There's a GM who will begin a job hunt shortly.

The second scenario is a parent who confronts the coach of his child's team. They've also just lost their fifth straight game. The coach offers the same cliché, "It's not whether you win or lose, it's how you play the game."

The confrontation by the parent in the second scenario should seem as absurd as the response of the GM in the first scenario. Yet, recreation league coaches will hear the grumbling of parents who think winning is a prerequisite for a successful season.

Youth sports provide a wonderful forum to teach children about rules-both rules of the game and "rules" of how to compete. When youth sports coaches bend or break the rules, they are sending the message that they don't respect these rules. When they argue with game officials, employ intimidation tactics, or use illegal equipment, they are teaching children how to connive at best, or worse, to outright cheat.

Coach Eddie encouraged children to use their size and momentum to run into defensive players, hoping for a dropped ball or to break up a double play. He encouraged them to "accidentally" kick the opponent covering a base so that the kicked child would fear being hurt again and shy away from the base on the next play. When they recapped after a game, the discussion was often about the pain they had inflicted and how it made the intended victim cry. Coach Eddie taught his players to be mean-spirited. He called this healthy aggression. What was done was just plain mean, and that's not what children should be learning.

Fortunately, most coaches do play within the rules and try to teach what is, and what is not, appropriate behavior. This kind of coaching encourages children to do their best and that is all anyone can ask of them. It's all we can ask of ourselves. That's what little league competition is all about.

FOR PARENTS AND COACHES: HOW TO COMPETE

Are children being taught to compete with themselves, to improve their skills and try their best? Are they being taught to enjoy victories because they indicate improved skills or because they've merely outscored an opponent?

VII: PARTICIPATION

Closely related to the four precepts categorized under the chapter, "Code of Behavior" are the following four precepts that relate more to involvement:

Setting Goals
Teamwork
Being Fair
Leadership

Coaches, parents, and those involved in youth sports need to recognize the need for children to learn the importance of working together in a manner that not only provides opportunities for the children to establish individual and team goals but also to build leadership skills through fair play.

Setting Goals – *18ᵗʰ precept*

"Our deeds determine us, as much as we determine our deeds." – George Eliot

Having goals gives children something to strive for. It creates ambition and affords them a sense of direction. Children will set goals themselves, however, their goals might not always be realistic ones, so you will need to help them set practical individual goals.

The best goals usually won't show up as a statistic at the end of the game. It might be a first catch or a first hit instead of the number of RBI's, goals or assists. Even more basic, since many very young kids will stand at the plate and watch the balls pass by, simply swinging the bat is a good initial goal. For first-time young soccer players, merely getting a foot on the ball might be a worthwhile goal. That first touch might even be the reason why the child returns the next year. Once that initial feat is achieved, his goals will develop as his skills and confidence mature.

Mom! Dad! Did you see me? I kicked it!

If you enjoy watching children at play, watch five-year-olds play soccer. Bob tells of his son, Josh's, soccer game. Although it was the last game of the season, the emphasis was not on winning. Josh and his teammates played hard, had riotous fun and as a reward for their efforts, were treated to pizza. There were unabashed smiles and giggles from all the children. Winning the World Cup would not have made them any happier. To Josh, pizza was the highlight of the season. That day Josh set a goal for himself. The following year he would play soccer again, and at the end of the season he would share pizza with his teammates.

Of course, as Josh gets older, his goals will change. Young children have such simple goals and that's as it should be. Proper perspective is necessary when setting goals for children. Consider if Josh's coach had set a goal of winning the championship instead of having fun and learning the game. Would Josh have set the same goal of playing soccer the next year? Perhaps, but the memory of fun and having pizza with his buddies is very enticing to a five-year-old, and increases the possibility that Josh will return, far more than if the emphasis had been on winning.

Explore the capabilities of your children and then help them set practical goals that can be achieved. The key is to understanding your children's skills as well as understanding their personal expectations. An enthusiastic "great single, Johnny" might be demeaning to Johnny if he was expecting, and fully capable of, a double. On the other hand, the same enthusiastic "great single, Mary" might be an appropriate response, if Mary's skills and goals were more limited.

It is important to set your children up for success. Unrealistic or unattainable goals create a stage for failure. Skill-based goals, individually tailored, can enhance self-esteem once achieved. Be sure to recognize goals as they are met and to replace satisfied goals with new ones to continue the path to success.

FOR PARENTS AND COACHES: SETTING GOALS

At the beginning of the season have each player set an objective for himself and write it down. It may simply be to catch one fly ball or to get a single assist. For the especially skilled player, instead of obvious goals like MVP or scoring leader, perhaps you can suggest that he set the worthy goal of making his teammates look good in every game? That gifted athlete might end up MVP after all, and will have achieved the honor in a selfless fashion while learning new skills in teamwork, sportsmanship, and leadership.

When a child succeeds in reaching his goal, applaud that success. Make a big deal of it. That child needs to feel a sense of accomplishment for having the necessary motivation and perseverance. As a coach, when you acknowledge the achievement, you are contributing to the development of that child in a most positive manner by creating a memory that will stay with him for years to come. Once a goal is achieved, have the child set another practical goal in consideration of his current improved abilities. With one success comes another, and another, and yet another, so that for many years he will still be setting and achieving realistic goals.

Teamwork – *3rd precept*

"No man can be provident of his time who is not prudent in the choice of his company." – Jeremy Taylor

Having just discussed the importance of individual players establishing personal goals, attention now shifts to working together as a unit to set and achieve team goals. This can get tricky. You want players to understand that the achievement of their own goals is important, but you also want them to work as a whole for the benefit of the team. Teaching one lesson does not have to diminish the value of the other.

Naturally, with teamwork, the more players who exhibit it, the better the team will perform. In making the team look good, individuals can themselves shine. Children soon learn others can help them achieve their individual goals and that they, in return, can help their teammates. This is evident when even a youth player will point his finger or give the high five to his teammate who made the pass that resulted in a goal, or otherwise made him look good. Children are able to see the results when individuals set aside their personal aspirations for the good of the whole team. With the proper guidance, they may be made aware that their best interests are served by helping the others on the team achieve a common outcome.

Learning the attribute of unselfishness is another one of life's valuable lessons. Personal qualities children learn about the team concept can carry over years later to their workplace, their marriage, and their family.

The coach's job entails teaching children that the team is not dependent upon a single individual to win the game any more than it is the fault of a single individual if the team loses. Every mom, dad, and grandparent sitting in the stands is there only to see their little one. They often stay so focused on their child that they frequently overlook the team concept. Although well meaning, they may yell "shoot" when their child nears the goal, neglecting to see another child has a better position. The coach may be yelling "pass" while parents shout conflicting instructions. These common scenarios place children in a no-win situation. Verbal encouragement is both recommended and beneficial to the kids trying hard to do their best. That holler is a natural way to elevate the efforts of your child. But when the hollers are instructions that conflict with the coach's strategy, naturally it confuses the children.

Another predicament that conflicts with teamwork arises from caring parents encouraging their children with monetary rewards. Money offered to kids for a homerun, a goal or other personal achievements is often disastrous to the team concept. For example, this might result in the quarterback of a peewee football team keeping the ball, rather than following the play with a pass. A little leaguer may try to hit the ball over the fence instead of just going for a single that would score the winning run. Imagine in junior pro basketball, a point guard's parent offering money for each basket he makes. Equally preposterous would be a parent offering a cash reward to their child-goalie for shooting at the open net during the last few seconds of a game instead of smothering the puck.

So how do you handle these situations, Coach? Those are times when you feel like screaming "what the *%#@* are you doing?" both to let off steam and to save face by letting other parents know that that was not how you designed the play. But yelling what you sometimes feel like yelling is not an option. Coaches should not be concerned with saving face because any parent knows that what children do is not always a reflection of how they were told to behave.

The solution to the well-meaning, but ill-informed parent problem is not so obvious and differs with each situation. At least the parents are showing some concern for the kid. Thousands of kids across the country are not playing youth sports because their parents could not, or did not, register them. Thousands of others are enrolled, but receive no support for the sport from home. Every team has that child who never touches his glove between practices. Some children on your team may go all season without a parent watching him play. So, instead of that harsh talk with the parent to inform him of your philosophy, consider that at least this is a parent who is trying to assist in making his child successful.

This may be one of those opportunities to tactfully educate a well-meaning, but misguided parent. Sometimes the best person to talk with that parent might be the child. Post-game talks could include reminders to the children to thank their parents for being there and for cheering for them, but that during games the team needs to be focused on listening to the coaches. Although never recommended, if bargaining is how the parent "helps" his child, the child might suggest that instead of that dollar for each homerun, how about a quarter for each time he was otherwise successful at the plate? Now, the parents and the coaches are working toward the same goal and it opens familial dialogue while providing an opportunity for the child to show the parent what he is learning about the sport. For instance, a child may be able to explain to a mother who isn't football savvy, that instead of intercepting a pass, he intentionally knocked it down because it was fourth down. The little league hitter might explain that his purpose at the plate was to advance a runner, and his caught fly ball was still successful and within the coaches' instructions.

Convincing kids (and sometimes parents) that while personal individual goals are important, they need to be implemented for the good of the team as a whole. Both kids and parents can be egocentric without realizing it. Constant subtle reminders stress the importance that all the individuals together make a team.

Many coaches teach team concepts with clichés and slogans such as "there is no 'I' in 'team'", and "T-E-A-M = Together Everyone Achieves More". "Team" is a popular huddle-breaking chant.

Every once in a while an athlete comes along who sometimes dominates a game due to superior physical size, strength or coordination, but even those individuals must learn to perform within the framework of the team. A single player cannot possibly win a game alone and, inevitably, the day will come when he will compete with others who are just as good, or better, than he is. Although it might be easy to overlook teaching team concepts to those superior young athletes, they are the ones who could benefit the most from learning teamwork skills.

One year Coach Eddie acquired a particularly gifted pitcher, Jim, whose abilities far surpassed the average for recreational league. Jim threw one shutout after another, striking out most batters who faced him. Coach Eddie used Jim in every game, in every inning. During one game, with the score 15 - 0, the opposing team's coach asked Coach Eddie to replace Jim so his team could get a few runs and have some fun, as the win was already assured. He refused. "You coach your team and I'll coach mine," he snapped back. What did Coach Eddie's team learn about teamwork that year? One can only guess what his reasons were, but Jim never played again after that year.

If our children learn to understand and work within the group dynamic at a young age, they will be masters of collaboration in their adult lives. Our personal lives and communities can benefit from our early teamwork lessons. Children will reap the many benefits of teamwork, among them the comfort of peer approval, the satisfaction that comes from feeling part of a group, and the delight of working towards a common goal. We are, after all, social creatures who crave the company of others.

FOR PARENTS AND COACHES: TEAMWORK

While individual goals are essential, be mindful to ensure that all the children work together, appreciate their teammates' contributions, and share in the joy of team and individual accomplishments. Be aware of any player who acts like he doesn't fit in. How can you include him in team activities to make him feel more like a part of the group?

Being Fair – *5th precept*

"One man's word is no man's word; we should quietly hear both sides." – Goethe

Today's child, if surrounded by fairness, is tomorrow's adult who upholds justice.

A truly fair situation can only be achieved through objective eyes, and that is, perhaps, the most difficult part of being human. We can't always see things through unbiased eyes because we are subjective beings. We base our opinions, our judgments and our actions on our own perspective-as we see things. Perception affects reality.

When Coach Eddie was asked to replace his unstoppable pitcher, Jim, in a mercy situation, he refused. In his mind his decision was the right one. He had a star pitcher and he would use him. Period! To Coach Eddie, fairness was not an issue, not even a consideration. So, Jim continued to pitch every inning, and the game was a bore to watch and to play-no one had fun. Even Jim, himself, decided not to play any more after that year. But Coach Eddie got to be the hero because his team "slaughtered" the other teams. It didn't occur to him that he was a hero in his eyes only.

David versus Goliath. Fear versus arrogance. Honestly, who is having fun?

As a coach, one of your greatest challenges is to be fair. What would you do if you found yourself with an outstanding talent on your team? The overzealous efforts of parents and coaches to capitalize on the talents of the gifted athlete is not only unfair to the rest of the team, it is unfair to that child too.

In some recreation leagues, that very talented player might be able to move up an age level. Or the child may want to play on a select team, and bypass the recreation league, in cities where that is a practical option. Those are decisions that should be made with the child's best interest in mind. Continuing in a league where he is unchallenged does not provide growth opportunities for the superstar.

Many years ago, in Brantford, Ontario, there was a young hockey talent. His skill was so superior that he played in higher age divisions his entire youthful career. This kept his skills challenged and created a fair situation for everyone. His skills were so exceptional that he went on to set dozens of National Hockey League records. This talent, Wayne Gretzky, illustrates an extreme example, but the principle is still applicable to youth sports.

What if Gretzky had been forced to play at his own age level? Worse still, what if there had been a Coach Eddie in his life? Like Jim, he might have lost interest in the game and quit playing forever!

Being fair is the one precept that will challenge your role as a coach the most. Satisfying some parents' curiosity as to why your best team isn't always utilized is sometimes a trying experience. Parents are there for a very different reason than you are. You are the leader, the teacher, the "Coach".

The following letter from Dan, in Seattle, Washington, clearly illustrates a lack of fairness and the long-term negative effects it can have on a child.

When I was in the seventh grade I went out for little league baseball. The coach of the team saw his role like that of a major league manager. His job was to win. Since we had recently moved, the coach didn't know who I was or what I could do, so I sat on the bench for three straight games. At each of the three games my father asked when I would get to play and reminded the coach about the purpose of little league ball. Each time he was told I would get to play soon.

During the fourth game my father confronted the coach near the end of the game and demanded I be put in the game. There was a strong atmosphere of physical threat in the confrontation. The coach snarled and put me in the game. Since everyone present had witnessed the altercation, I was the center of attention. All conversation stopped and every eye was on me as I stood terrified at the plate. I struck out on the first three pitches and immediately quit the team.

As things turned out, I was a very good athlete and I love baseball. However, I never played ball again. I'm in my late forties now and have always regretted the baseball I never got to play because of this one incident.

Dan's trauma is over thirty years old, yet even in his late forties he still remember the humiliation as though it were yesterday. One very misguided coach directly affected the life of another human being by losing sight of what fair play is all about.

Kids cannot learn fairness until they experience it themselves. Dan's memory could have and should have been a very different one. If you think a child will forget being treated unfairly by the team's victory, please read his letter again.

Gerry Crowley

FOR PARENTS AND COACHES: BEING FAIR

Do you manage not only the individuals, but also the team as a whole, in a manner that promotes fairness? Are disputes resolved fairly and in children's best interests, or are adult politics affecting the children? On a larger scale, is fairness part of the league's organizational mandate and rules?

Leadership – *10th precept*

> *"I am not a teacher: only a fellow-traveler of whom you asked the way. I pointed ahead-ahead of myself as well as of you."* – *George Bernard Shaw*

There are followers and there are leaders. Is it possible for a follower to turn into a leader? Sean, from Massachusetts, answers that question with a memory from his childhood.

"I was in the forth or fifth grade and playing some form of dodge ball at recess. We had mothers as recess monitors. It was general practice for those of us not as athletically inclined as others to surrender the ball to the 'best' player on the team if we happened to get hold of it. This practice benefited the team because the best player had a much better chance of getting an 'out'. The obvious problem is that it reduced children like myself to the status of water boy.

One particular day I got the ball and looked for the 'best' player to pass it to. As I stood, searching, the recess monitor asked me what I was doing. I told her I was looking for the 'best player'. 'THROW THE BALL YOURSELF,' was her instant and loud reply.

*I have no idea what happened then. I do know I threw the ball, and I do know I never again gave it to the 'best player'. I am totally without recollection of the outcome of the play. I only know that I threw it **myself**!*

I played two sports in high school, captained my soccer team in college and went on to be an NCAA Division II head coach. I have been in leadership positions all my life and I have always remembered that moment. How would my life have turned out had she not yelled at me to throw the ball? I say a resounding 'Thank you, recess mother', and wish that I could thank her today. If all of us could have the same clear vision … 'just play the game and do your best' …what a wonderful time the children of all ages would have. What a great generation of leaders we could raise!

…a moment that Sean will remember forever.

A moment of chance and Sean's life was changed forever. In an instant his leadership skills became apparent. A stranger gave Sean a choice he never realized he had, and it became a turning point of his life.

Parents and coaches have many opportunities to be a "recess monitor" hero. That *ah-ha* moment could come in a variety of ways, but none is as powerful as occurring while bringing out the leadership skills of a child. Not all children will become NCAA coaches like Sean, but they all have areas where they will excel.

Leadership can easily be defined as the ability to guide others. That makes us all leaders. As parents, teachers, aunts, uncles, singers, actors, radio announcers, sports heroes, and, of course, youth sports coaches, we all touch the lives of children on a daily basis. Therefore, it is important to think about the different kinds of leadership and what children respond to best. The first place to start is by setting the best possible example. Children exemplify the saying, "monkey see, monkey do".

Coach Eddie is not alone in the way he coaches. During a little league championship tournament game, another coach, "John", displayed a perfect example of how *not* to lead children.

The situation was a "must win" for both teams – one would advance and the other would be eliminated. Late in the game there were two close plays at first base, and both were called outs against John's team. John went berserk. He screamed. He cursed. He flailed his arms about. As if a cue by the coach for the little leaguers to join in, the children followed John's behavior by shouting insults and obscenities of their own. The situation worsened when John, who knew this was likely his last game of the season, picked up first base and tossed it in the direction of the umpire shouting, "Here, take a close look what the base looks like." Mimicking their coach, the children began throwing things – their hats, equipment, towels, and water bottles. When the coach remained out-of-control, the children began to stomp on the items they had thrown and not knowing what to do next, some even threw themselves on the ground and cried. John was ejected. As he left the park, he pointed to the young players following his lead and once again screamed at the umpire, "See what you've done to the kids?"

A week later, the League suspended John from coaching for two years. Unfortunately, the damage had been done. During the incident, the players did not envision that the behavior of all involved would be viewed so negatively later. Some parents did not realize it either, as a few had joined in the bedlam of the ugly incident. Those parents had an opportunity to display positive leadership that day and missed it.

The responsibilities of leadership don't begin and end with the coach. Parental leadership, too, is essential at the games in which your child is participating. Children often hear their parent's voice above all others in the crowd. During an incident like the one at that final game of the season, what will the voice from the bleachers that your child hears be saying? When your child glances at you to see your reaction, what will he see?

The way you react to a perceived bad call sends a very clear message to your child. If you rant and rave and blame others, if you denigrate the official, then you have done harm by teaching a bad lesson. Children carry negative lessons with them throughout their lives. They'll get "bad calls" with test grades, in personal relationships, and on the job. How they handle injustices throughout their lives is largely shaped by how coaches and parents deal with inequities.

Fortunately, most parents take the ups and downs of the game in stride, not getting too upset over decisions made by umpires or referees, choosing, instead, to seize the opportunity to display appropriate leadership skills. Coaches, parents, and other authority figures in children's lives must always be mindful of the example they set through their own displays of leadership.

FOR PARENTS AND COACHES: LEADERSHIP

Children develop good leadership characteristics by participating in activities that involve adults who are good leaders themselves. Think back to your own childhood. Were your primary caregivers good leaders? ... what about those secondary role models-grandparents, teachers, and coaches? ... and those adults who may have influenced your life for short periods-scout leaders, Sunday School teachers, or babysitters. Were you fortunate to have an outstanding leader in your life? Do you now see any of those people in yourself?

VIII: DEVELOPMENT OF SKILLS

Physical Skills
Learning the Game
Physical Fitness

It was not surprising that when asked, "What do you want the coach to teach your children?" that physical skills, learning the game and physical fitness were 2nd, 4th, and 12th, on the list. It just makes sense that a parent would want to see his child acquire the physical skills of the game, learn the rules, and get some exercise.

Physical Skills – *2nd precept*

> *"The dwarf see farther than the giant, when he has the giant's shoulders to mount on." – Coleridge*

Teaching physical skills is a step-by-step process. Each child progresses through those steps at different rates, depending on factors such as his current skills set, his motivation, the time he works on skills outside of practice, and outside influences in his life. Coaches love the "coachable" kids – the players who are good listeners, have good attitudes, do as directed, and show improvement. What's a challenge for coaches is to teach those less-than-coachable ones. Every coach has had the child with tremendous talent, but whose bad attitude or poor attendance hinders his achievements. The troubled child's issues likely stem from other aspects of the child's life, but just manifest themselves with the team. While trying to teach this child the physical skills required of the game, realize that he possibly has some basic needs of life that are not being met. It is difficult for this child to concentrate, display good sportsmanship, and be receptive to your efforts. Find comfort knowing that the attention you give this child might be much more critical to his overall development than his acquisition of new sports skills.

To assist with instructing the rest of the team, who come ready to learn and have fun, there are plenty of how-to-coach books available with tips on teaching the physical skills of whatever sport you're coaching. Even veteran coaches could benefit by reviewing a how-to manual. Both the easy-to-coach and the hard-to-coach children respond best to instruction that's sincere and caring, rather than loud and intimidating.

Coaches need to create an environment of positive learning, not one in which the child is afraid to make a mistake. Always remember that the emotional state of a child is a very fragile thing. Children who are not afraid to make mistakes have a significant advantage, whereas those who are taught through a punishment system of doing push-ups, running around the field, skating around the rink, sitting on the bench, will drown in a pool of insecurity. Children learn best by hands-on repetitive practice in addition to verbal instructions. The "rule of six" indicates that even adults have to hear something six times before we remember it, so repetition cannot be underestimated with a child, especially where eye-hand coordination and physical skills are coupled with memory. It is that repetition that transforms actions into desired habits. As children learn new skills, they thrill in the process itself. Their self-esteem comes from doing the best they possibly can, not from your perception of perfection. You must encourage the effort, not necessarily the action.

It's a natural tendency for us to want to do what we're good at. A little leaguer who's a long-ball hitter will enjoy batting practice and will likely respond well to advice designed to help him hit even further. The coach will assist him at his advanced level while helping him realize that having physical skills is not only about hitting well.

If coaches of young children let parents know what particular skill they are developing during practice, perhaps during play times at home, the parents could work with their children on that latest skill. Parents appreciate being informed because it enables them to further participate in the development of their children.

The ideal situation is having the parents "on the same page" with the coach. If their philosophies contrast, it is usually because they have different values. Parents assisting their children at home will not bridge conflicting value systems, but it may help the parent understand why the coach is emphasizing particular skill sets.

The following conversation between Wayne Campbell, a coach of ten-year-old baseball players, and a parent reflects such a situation.

"How did the team do today?"

"The team did great! As you know, we practiced all week long how to place the feet when trying to bunt. During the game each child stood perfectly. I'm so proud of them. We really learned something today. It's a great feeling. It's what keeps me coaching."

"But did we win?!"

"You know, I'm not really sure. I'm so pleased that the kids learned to bunt so well, I never even thought of whether we won or lost the game."

How refreshing it is to encounter a coach so wrapped up in the development of physical skills that he considers the score unimportant. Coach Campbell's philosophy was to teach and sharpen physical skills with little focus on the outcome of each game. All of his practices emphasized developing new skills and practicing skills already learned. Once players had mastered a skill, they would assist those who needed a little extra help. At games the players put these new skills to work. Coach Campbell's players were taught that making mistakes is part of the game. When errors occurred they were encouraged to try again, which created fearless determination during games. Like all good coaches, Coach Campbell recognized that players develop physical skills not only at practice, but also during games. He structured the games to create an atmosphere where each child was able to try out new skills. What did the kids think? The next year at registration, many of the children who had been coached by Coach Campbell made a special notation on their registration form. It read, "Please put me on Coach Campbell's team!" That notation by the kids pretty much says it all.

Unfortunately, coaches like Wayne Campbell are a rare breed. Too many are like Coach Eddie. A typical practice for Coach Eddie was to pick his four best players and put them in the infield. For nearly an hour Coach Eddie hit ball after ball to each of his luminaries, practicing every conceivable variation on an infield play in preparation for the next game they would win. Errors were not tolerated.

The rest of the team was ushered to the outfield where parents who happened to be on hand hit fly balls to them for nearly the entire practice. Coach Eddie paid little attention to teaching new skills to his weak players, the ones who needed it the most. Children who are trying to learn new skills need to hear: *"Awesome catch", "Great try", "That's wonderful", "Wow, you sure are improving", "Look at you!"* Receiving good instruction on basic physical skills is imperative for the development of the young athlete and for his enjoyment and appreciation of the sport.

Millions of children participate in physical activities that they can do their entire lives, such as swimming, running, walking, tennis, golf, softball, bowling, cycling, dance, etc. Kids deserve a good coach, one who will teach the basic skills used in the sport and correct bad habits the youngsters display. Physical skills needed to learn a new sport are best learned at a young age. Just ask any middle-aged first-time snow skier!

FOR PARENTS AND COACHES: PHYSICAL SKILL

Consider whether the physical skills of individual children are being improved and made an important part of practices and games. Are the children equally encouraged and provided with appropriate and useful age-appropriate skills improvement plans that are simple and fun to institute?

Learning The Game – *4th precept*

"…live to learn…" – Bayard Taylor

"The real character of a man is found out by his amusement."
- Sir Joshua Reynolds

Similar to varying skill abilities, children will arrive with different levels of game awareness. Some may not even know the basic rules of the sport. Others will know the rules, the tricks-of-the-trade, and have natural sports instincts.

Because the players on any team have a variety of abilities and knowledge, it is important to have a roadmap of where you want your team to be at the end of the year. What skills should they have learned? To what extent should they know the rules of the game? Use the answers to those questions as a guide to plan your practices. Mix up the agenda to add variety to the practice. They should learn rules in conjunction with the skill that they're learning. For example, when your T-ballers are learning how to steal bases, explain that they cannot lead off the bases like they've seen their big brothers do in higher leagues. Teach them about a rule you haven't paired with a skill, or rules you want to reinforce, when they're resting after physical exercise. Use rainy days as an opportunity to review rules, if you have a recreation building, an office, a shelter, or even a dugout available. Instead of only using a lecturing format, quiz the children on rules they've learned and let them participate in the learning process.

Having a pre-planned outline of your roadmap allows you to introduce and implement new skills and rules in an orderly fashion keeping you on track with your agenda. It helps you and your assistants prepare for practices.

Don't bombard them with too many details at once. Even adults have limits on the amount of information they can process in one sitting. Children's attention spans are much shorter – probably shorter than we realize.

When teaching rules, be sure that your players understand which rules are league rules and which rules are game policies. For example, the little league football player should be able to learn that in some incidences blocking below the waist will draw a penalty (a rule violation), but blocking someone other than his designated assignment will be a breach of instructional rules – (not a rule violation and no penalty). Children should be taught how some common rules (like pass interference) are different at varying levels; peewee, high school, college, and pro football have different rules for the same situation.

In order to achieve the goal of this precept-to learn the game, remember to speak the language of the children you coach. Coaches are facilitators of learning. Design plays that your children can easily remember. Designing difficult or elaborate plays, inconsistent with their age or ability, creates a situation where failure is inevitable. Start with simple strategies and progress to each level accordingly. Create plays they can visualize rather than relying on memory alone.

It is important that children realize that as long as they continue to participate that learning the game is a continuous education.

FOR PARENTS AND COACHES: LEARNING THE GAME

Are practices broken down into age-appropriate and skill-developing areas? Are practices enjoyable, full of learning and fun? Is practice kept within reasonable limits in terms of the age group and desire of the children? Is the game being taught in a clear, logically expanding and understandable way?

Physical Fitness – *12ᵗʰ precept*

> *"Man is of soul and body, formed for deeds…" - Shelley*

Whereas the first section in this chapter, "Physical Skills", deals with attaining the aptitudes to perform an action, "physical fitness" refers to the overall state of health of the child. The mastering of physical skills is more easily achieved when the physical fitness of the child is good. It is not unusual for young gifted athletes to be talented in multiple sports. A common trait of multi-talented children is their superior physical fitness.

The human body is truly a remarkable piece of work, in repose and especially in action. Ours bodies can bend, jump, twist, turn, run, and roll. We were made for physical movement. In fact, our very health, mental and physical, is directly linked to exercise. Evidence suggests that our self-image is dependent upon participation in some kind of physical activity.

What is fitness? How important is it? Is it physical or psychological?

Fitness is the state of being in suitable condition to do something, and that can be physical, mental or both. Whether you are preparing for an exam in school, or for the decathlon, the more prepared you are, the better your chance to excel. Its importance is aptly described by James Michener in his book *Sports in America:*

I believe that children, like little animals, require play and competition in order to develop. I believe that play is a major agency in civilizing infants. I believe that big muscle movement helps the infant establish his balance within the space in which he will henceforth operate. I believe that competition, reasonably supervised, is essential to the full maturing of the individual."

Michener is not alone in his belief that each child must develop physically in order to obtain good health in mind and body. According to Dr. Eric Margenau, psychologists agree that movement of the muscles creates body awareness, which leads to a sense of self-assurance and control.

Therefore, it is important to prepare children for a given task-game, race, etc.-to ensure that they don't incur injury and will be able to perform at their optimum. Regardless of physical abilities, pre-game calisthenics are essential. Small children certainly don't require the same warm-up period the adults do, but getting them used to the routine will develop a good life-long habit.

When we watch sporting events on television, we don't see the pre-game exercises that the athletes perform, so children are not aware that even their heroes exercise before each and every game. A child's natural exuberance pushes him to get right into the game with one hundred percent effort, but without proper warm-up they risk long-term injury which could plague them for the rest of their lives. A simple routine of exercises before each activity can prevent such injury.

It is the coach's job to encourage children to show up ten minutes early and stretch those little arms and legs. To that end, it's a good idea for each coach to familiarize himself with a variety of exercises associated with the game they're coaching. Libraries carry many books of this nature and there are also videotapes and CD's available on every sport. Most regions across the country hold coaching clinics, which can be very helpful. In fact, it should be mandatory for any coach to attend these clinics.

Remember that it's not enough just to have the little ones run around the field a couple of times. While this is good for their cardiovascular health, it doesn't stretch specific muscles that they'll be using during the activity.

FOR PARENTS AND COACHES: PHYSICAL FITNESS

Are the children taught to warm up and cool down before and after strenuous activity? Is practice time dedicated to overall fitness of the children, including cardiovascular fitness, or is practice dedicated only to specific game skills? Is part of the goal of the children's work with their teams to gently improve fitness? Is fitness part of an overall strategy to keep injury to children to a minimum? Is fitness and health part of the mandate of your organization?

IX: PSYCHOLOGICAL FACTORS

W e've all heard the sayings, "Get your game face on", "Get your head into it", "Be tough", "Get into the game", "Stay focused", "Be ready", and other clichés that address the players' frame of mind. The following four precepts deal with the psychological part of the game-a much bigger part of the game than you might think.

Discipline/Self Control
Motivation
Patience
Resilience

Discipline and Self-Control – *7ᵗʰ precept*

"You cannot teach a man anything; You can only help him to find it within himself." – Galileo

A twelve-year-old is racing toward the goal, soccer ball at his feet. With mounting excitement at the thrill of his impending third goal playing in his mind, he is tripped by an opposing player. No penalty is called-the ref missed it. The twelve-year-old gets up and angrily kicks the ball, swearing at the defending player. A scuffle breaks out and, because he initiated the fight, he is ejected from the game. His team loses. The coach, teammates and parents are enraged with the referee.

Sadly, that anger is all they'll all take away with them from that game. The referee missed a tripping call. Officials at all levels miss calls and they always will. Somewhere along the way that twelve-year-old learned to channel his frustration into rage. Fighting is a learned behavior and we need to look to our own conduct as the source. If we don't teach self-discipline by example, how can we expect it of our children or those we guide?

After the game the young official acknowledged that he missed the call and felt terrible about it. Yet he couldn't understand why the adults were so rude to him. This scenario is all too common and illustrates the lack of discipline in many sports today.

Coach Eddie would not have found the actions of the coach, or the spectators, or even the player, out of place under the circumstances. He believes he knows all about discipline. If you make a mistake on Coach Eddie's team, you do ten push-ups. If you make the same mistake again, you run laps around the field. If you don't live up to his expectations, you'll find yourself getting splinters on the bench. Someone once asked Coach Eddie why he benched a player who had struck out. He replied, "When I was a kid that's how my coach disciplined me when I struck out. It worked, because I still remember it. The kid will never forget, will he?"

He is absolutely right. That child will never forget. It won't improve his batting, and he'll face the next at-bat with fear of failure, but he surely won't forget. The fact is, if you look at the incident, there isn't a single positive lesson to be learned from Coach Eddie's methods. All he is offering is negative reinforcement.

Most adults can remember a time from their childhood where the punishment is remembered long after the perceived infraction has been forgotten. It behooves every coach to ask himself what kind of influence he has on the kids' ability to practice self-control.

Discipline is not about anger and punishment. It is about training the mind and developing character. Self-control must come from within the individual, but it is a coachable attribute. Learning to control temper and developing inner strength to rise above difficulties are stepping-stones to acquiring self-discipline.

Stay positive. Stick to your own agenda. Find the good in every situation. And soon you will see your young players being positive, following instructions, and not giving up. Self-control is contagious; it is taught through example. Kids will still need those occasional reminders that throwing equipment, criticizing teammates, and complaining to officials are all unacceptable. Having a clear understanding of team rules will help, as the most basic form of self-discipline is following instructions. The middle tier of self-discipline is controlling emotions, which can be taught by coaches and parents in sports and non-sports settings. The more sophisticated self-discipline issues involve the child's ability to analyze situations and determine the best course of action on his own. Being a part of a well-disciplined organization, whether it is a school, family unit, or sports team, can help provide the foundation for successful higher-level self-control.

FOR PARENTS AND COACHES: DISCIPLINE AND SELF-CONTROL

What kind of lessons about discipline and self-control are evident in the role models-the parents and coaches-in your organization? Are children being taught to control their tempers while expressing legitimate frustration in a civilized way? Is collaborative dispute resolution part of your organization's usual operation?

Motivation – *8th precept*

> *"Selfishness is the grand moving principle of nine-tenth of our actions." – La Rochefoucauld*

Motivation-simple in explanation, complex in execution. It is a factor that causes you to want to do something. Motivating others can be difficult. Motivation issues permeate every career. Salesmen try to motivate buyers. Pre-school teachers motivate their little ones. Businesses motivate lots of stakeholders-employees, shareholders, clients, and vendors. Each of these professionals deals with the same issues coaches and parents face with motivating youth in sports. Some of their buyers, students, stakeholders, and youth are easily influenced; others are not.

Coaches often have to resort to salesman-like techniques to motivate those players who lack an innate drive. Explaining results and consequences work for some of the hard-to-motivate kids. *"If you change your stance, you will hit the ball farther." "If you don't come to practice you will not learn the plays."* Those explanations work better for that difficult audience than *"If you execute properly, we will win."* Coaches must be prepared to be salesmen at times. Winning at all costs is generally ineffective motivation for unenthusiastic children, as they usually don't care about winning and losing. Winning at all costs is even ineffective motivation for the go-getters on your team because they often have a higher sense of accomplishment. They want to do better so they'll make all-stars, or they are natural leaders, or they just like to compete.

When dealing with motivational issues, coaches have to be creative. Each child is motivated by different desires. Finding what makes each one tick can be tricky. What may enhance the performance in one child might hinder the performance of another. For example, pointing out how pleased the parents must be to one child who is showing improvement might be very encouraging, but to that child whose parents would prefer he play a different sport, motivation along that line might not be so fitting.

Parents' comments can have a tremendous effect of the motivation of the child. As previously discussed in the teamwork precept of Chapter 7, parents need to be mindful that their comments are consistent with the team goals. The child who receives conflicting messages will be confused and might be harder to motivate the next time he receives advice from a parent or coach.

It is a natural tendency to do things that bring pleasure. Coaches who make their sports fun have the upper hand in motivation. Their children want to repeat what was fun. *Wanting to* is the key to motivation!

Coach Eddie thought he was a good motivator. He forced team members who made mistakes to apologize to teammates. To further drive home his point, he benched the offenders. Children should never leave a game thinking that they caused their team to lose, or that they are not integral to the team. This kind of action instills fear and resentment. Intimidation is a poor long-term motivator.

...he can sit on the bench for the rest of the year for all I care...

Coaches should continually monitor what effect their motivational techniques have on the players. Those coaches who successfully motivate the wide range of talent and emotional capacities on a youth sports team are truly the masters of winning without winning.

FOR PARENTS AND COACHES: MOTIVATION

Is effort rewarded and recognized? Are all children included and encouraged?

Is coaching in your organization impatient and easily frustrated with the sincere efforts of children? Are children given the time they need to learn?

Patience – *13th precept*

"He that can have patience can have what he will." –
Franklin

Teach children tolerance and they will grow up patient.

Patience. Every day of our lives things happen that tests our patience and each of us reacts differently. Think about your own degree of patience-it's crucial to your coaching-but it's difficult to assess.

Say you are driving along a two-way highway. The car in front of you is doing the posted speed limit, but you want to go faster. You think about passing. If you're a patient driver, you'll pass when it is safe to do so. If you are not, you'll pass at will, presuming it is safe. Which driver are you?

You're standing in a long line-up at the ATM, the theatre, a restaurant, the bank, or even the ice cream parlor. Each person in that line will respond to the wait with varying degrees of patience. Some will take the wait in stride, talking and laughing the moments away, while others will become visibly agitated. They mumble, they grumble, and they annoy others around them. By the time their turn arrives, anger and frustration are in control. Which sort of person are you?

We all have our own comfort zone-and a pace that suits our personality, whether at work or play. Yet, now and then circumstances arise which force us to move either a little faster or a little slower. How we react is a test of our patience, our inner tranquillity. Children, too, have their own pace at which they do things, and some children learn more quickly than others do.

In school, teachers often display an incredible amount of patience with students who take a little longer to grasp new concepts. It's something good teachers work very hard to develop, understanding its benefit to the students. A patient teacher knows she will experience success in the end, whereas one who is less patient will turn the lesson into an exercise in frustration for everyone involved.

Little league coaches are also teachers. They, too, interact with children, teaching them new skills, and being the best role model they can be. Yet, many times, there seems to be a significant difference. When a school teacher has a student who is experiencing a particularly difficult time with some new skill, she will work longer and harder with that one student, even granting him extra time on her lunch hour, or after school, in order to help that child catch up. Conversely, when a coach experiences a similarly difficult situation, he too often mistakenly believes that he can bully that child into learning. Instead of patiently giving more of his time, he will impatiently cast that child aside as unable to succeed, or worse, cause him to believe that he simply isn't trying hard enough.

Coach Eddie believes that coaching is very different from teaching. His desire to win leaves little room for tolerance. Coach Eddie is wrong, because he doesn't understand that winning isn't what it's about. The children are what it's about. They are little individuals whose bodies and minds are still developing. Boys and girls, whose emotions run close to the surface, are perceptively aware that coach doesn't treat each one the same. Little people who one day will be adults and will react to life using the tools they were given in childhood. What tools are you giving them?

I have no time for mistakes. Hmph. Maybe if I bully him, he will quit the team...

Patience is a very special quality. With it a person has the capacity to endure pain, troubles or hardships without complaint. Patience gives us the ability to persevere without losing heart or becoming bored. How many of our own decisions would have been different if we'd just had a little more patience? How patient are you as a coach?

FOR PARENTS AND COACHES: PATIENCE

Is coaching in your organization impatient and easily frustrated with the sincere efforts of the children? Are coaches kindly guides, or do they expect to behave like tyrants? Are children given the time they need to learn?

Resilience – *19th precept*

"We shall escape the uphill by never turning back."
- Christina G. Rossetti

We have all seen incidents that cause people to react in different ways. Some people get angry over the weather, while others simply take it in stride. Some wait patiently at a red light while others fume.

Have you ever wondered why some people become annoyed easily and others seem to possess the patience of Job? The child failed to score on a breakaway or perhaps struck-out with the tying run on third base. There are some parents who react with anger and shout at the child. But there are parents who react only with encouragement. What do you do?

People who remain calm in uncomfortable situations are confident that things will improve. They believe that misfortune, whether it is a rainy day, a red light, a missed goal, a strikeout or even a job setback, is only temporary. They will bounce back. They are resilient.

Children react differently, too, to given situations. Very young children usually just shrug off a mistake and carry on. They may not even realize that they have made a mistake until the coach tells them or someone yells at them. As children get older they recognize personal mistakes and when they do, they are hardest on themselves. In sports they feel dreadful about letting the team down. And a win-at-all-costs coach will make them feel even worse. All of a sudden the game becomes serious and the fun is gone.

Imagine you are a ten-year-old child excited about being in the game. Your parents are there watching for the very first time. It's your big moment to make the play, but, oh no, you make a mistake! You feel terrible about it. You want to cry, then Dad yells, *"It's okay! Get back in the game, John!"*

That's encouragement.

Coaches and parents alike need to be aware that what children need most when they make a mistake is support and encouragement. We have all heard the cliché, "If, at first, you don't succeed, try, try again." The message is one of resilience. A child who makes a mistake needs to learn from it, forget the negativity, and get on with the task at hand. Positive encouragement from the coach goes a long way to building confidence in children. Coaches must promote the idea that mistakes are learning experiences. Children who believe this won't be afraid to try new challenges. They will set higher goals for themselves. As children grow older and make mistakes-and they will make mistakes-chances are that they will shrug them off, just like they did when they were three years old. It's up to you to help create the resilience, which will lead to self-confidence.

Major league pitcher Jim Abbott, born without a right hand, is an excellent example of resilience. It would have been so easy for him to give up and play the victim his whole life. Instead he chose to persevere, and pursue his dream in spite of his so-called handicap. In 1987 he was the first baseball player to win the Sullivan Award as the nation's outstanding amateur athlete. He was the starting quarterback on his high school football team, which went to the finals of the Michigan State championship. On

September 4th, 1993, pitching for the New York Yankees he pitched a no-hitter against the Cleveland Indians. This is one man who likely received a hearty helping of support and encouragement in his formative years. He is a modern-day hero and a lesson to us all.

Terry Fox, who ran across Canada with only one leg, raising money for cancer research, is an example of supreme heroism. Rick Hansen, the Olympic cyclist who was paralyzed in an accident and who has dedicated his life to educating others about disabilities, has risen above events and transcended his accident. Olympic officials, recognizing Rick's resilience, chose him as one of the final torchbearers at the 2010 Winter Olympics in Vancouver BC.

An ultimate example of resilience is the actor, Christopher Reeve-Superman to millions of fans. When an equestrian accident left him with a broken neck, unable to move any part of his body, not able to breathe for himself, he did not want to go on living. Through the love, support and encouragement of his family, he came back more determined than ever. His struggle was not an easy one, each day being a trial of survival. Yet he signed contracts to direct after the accident happened. He was committed to going on with his life and his work, and to doing everything in his power to raise awareness and the necessary funding for spinal injury research. One must look at Mr. Reeve and say, "If this man can be so resilient after such a devastating injury, it is within every person's power to be so."

So Coach, the next time one of your charges makes a mistake, think about the above examples and support the child so he too can bounce back.

FOR PARENTS AND COACHES: RESILIENCE

Are children being taught resilience-the inner strength to bounce back-or are they being "toughened" in a way that make them rigid and impossibly perfectionist?

X: THE THREE R's

Closely related to the four precepts categorized under the chapter, "Code of Behavior", the following four precepts relate more to distinct involvement.

Respect
Reliability
Responsibility

Respect – *14th precept*

> *"A moral, sensible, and well-bred man will not affront me, and no other can - Cowper*

Within every person there is an extraordinary power. Most people live their entire lives and never realize the magic of that power, yet how one uses it might well determine one's destiny. It is so delicate a thing that a single negative incident can reduce that power to nothing. On the other hand, when used positively, it can move mountains.

That power is *respect*. Respect is not for sale, nor can you bully others into it, for, although many may defer to you, these polite displays are but ghosts of the real thing. How, then, do you gain the respect of others?

Coach Eddie believed that using fear of punishment would achieve his ultimate goal - to win. He mistakenly believed that the more games he won, the greater would be the respect people paid him, and the children were mere pawns in his personal pursuit. Fear and intimidation were tools he used to mould the children into obedience. He probably believed he had their respect.

One particular year, Coach Eddie was without a pitcher, so he called a child-star who had not signed up and offered to pay him to play. Yes, Coach Eddie offered a cash incentive for each win and each shutout. Coach Eddie probably believed he could buy the pitcher's respect.

There is no magical formula for earning the respect of the kids on your team, although earning is a good place to start. Once again, I'm going to compare coaching to teaching, where some of the best examples are set. I recently had a discussion with an elementary school French teacher, Christina, who also helps coach the school sports teams before class, during her lunch hour, and after school. Her programs, both in and out of the classroom, are incredibly successful and her popularity with the students is almost legendary. I asked her how she earned such respect from her students.

It's not something I think about. My students see how hard I work, the genuine interest I show for them and that my concern for their education and their well-being is sincere. I make sure that they feel they are worthy of my time. And, of course, I give them the same respect I expect from them. They will never hear me being sarcastic with them, and I will never, ever belittle them or their efforts. I take care never to underestimate them, and I show them my personal side so that they know my values, my beliefs, who I really am. They know I am human, and I'm not afraid to show them my fear, my anger, or my sadness."

In turn, her students give one hundred percent of themselves. Not only are they not afraid to try new skills, but they are proud to share with her the skills they have mastered. Most of her students would journey to the ends of the earth for her, such is their devotion for a teacher who respects them for who they are, not just for what they can do. She says her philosophy is simple. Achievement does not bring self-esteem-rather build self-esteem and that will bring achievement.

That same philosophy works in her coaching, as well. But, she cautions, the first place to start is with the sport itself.

A coach must be skilled, because a coach who is out of his depth will resort to anger and derision instead of critical analysis and decision. A good coach is going to know his players better than they know themselves. And they will trust him. They'll know that coach might put them into a difficult situation, but never an impossible situation. Like when Coach Mario Tremblay left Patrick Roy in net after he had let in something like nine goals. That should never have happened. Tremblay should have pulled Roy, and saved him the humiliation. I will never mould my students, or my players, through fear or guilt or intimidation!"

Through example, a good teacher, coach, or parent can make children understand that respect is a very special consideration, a special esteem in which one person holds another. Respect means many things: rising above controversy, standing firm with your convictions, removing yourself from a comfort zone in support of what is right, and ensuring children are learning what is right, in spite of what others do. These elements form the kind of respect that moves mountains.

FOR PARENTS AND COACHES:
RESPECT

Are the children respected as essential and important individuals in your organization and on their team? Is respect from the children for adults demanded and commanded rather than earned?

Reliability – *15ᵗʰ precept*

"To be relied upon is a great compliment than to be loved." -Anonymous

Have you ever made plans with someone who cancelled out at the last minute or simply didn't show up? What about you? Have you ever changed or cancelled a commitment because it wasn't convenient for you? When you tell friends that you'll pick them up at a certain time, or that you'll meet them at an appointed hour, are you there? Do you keep your promises?

It's so easy to believe that the others will understand your reasons for being unable to meet that commitment. You may even have convinced yourself that your decision is justified. It's an erroneous assumption. What you really need to be asking yourself is whether or not you are the kind of person others can count on. Be sure you are honest with yourself when you answer.

Reliable people are conscientious and trustworthy, honoring their commitments whenever humanly possible. They aren't likely to change plans because something better came along. In short, a reliable person can be relied upon by family, co-workers, friends, and even strangers.

Reliability is a quality that children learn through example. If the coach is late, or doesn't show up, anticipation and excitement turn to confusion and bewilderment. Why didn't the coach show up? Yet, if children are surrounded by adults that always honor their commitments, they will grow up understanding the need to keep their word. It's another one of those lessons that can be learned through coaching on the sports field, yet carries into all other aspects of their lives. Only through action can you demonstrate to them that you are reliable.

If you've made the decision to become a coach, be certain that you can make the time, because commitment requires time. You must be there ahead of the appointed hour for all games and all practices, and make the parents aware that part of their responsibility means that they, too, need to be reliable. Through this mutual example, the children can't help but get the right message. Make it clear to each member of your team that it is his responsibility to let the coach know if he is going to be late or unable to attend. All the talent in the world isn't worth dust if you are not reliable.

FOR PARENTS AND COACHES: RELIABILITY

Are the children encouraged by example to be reliable? Do coaches and parents act in consistently reliable ways?

Responsibility – *17ʰ precept*

> *"The things which must be, must be for the best, …to*
> *do our duty…humbly … " -Owen Meredith*

For the most part, the ideas contained in this book are based on my own observations and experiences with little league players and coaches, and I have used these for my arguments. Responsibility however is such an important part of life that it requires more in-depth reflection. Accepting responsibility is a vital part of any child's development and will determine the usefulness of their role within society.

Who *is* responsible for what a child learns? One might answer teachers, of course. But if we think about the different areas of learning, we must certainly look beyond teachers, for their influence on children is confined to a finite period of time. Yes, they teach the basics of reading, writing and arithmetic, and more specific skills and concepts as children progress to higher levels, and they work to instill a general code of ethics and moral behavior. But a teacher is just one of many who will walk through a child's life.

A child's well-being is the responsibility of parents or guardians, foremost. In supporting roles is an entire cast of individuals-relatives, friends, religious leaders, family doctors, and, of course, coaches. In fact, anyone who spends any amount of time with that child, anyone who the child views in a position of authority bears responsibility to that child-though admittedly the ultimate weight falls on the shoulders of the parents. Where your child is concerned, "the buck stops here".

We are living in an age of blame. We want someone to blame for all the ills of the world-crime, unemployment, poverty, environmental pollution, and social unrest and conflict. We blame television, the movies, newspapers, magazines, rock groups and government. We even blame each other.

After four consecutive days of rain, I overheard someone say, "That stupid weather girl said the sun would shine today, and it's raining again!" Is the weather announcer to blame for the rain?

It comes, then, as no surprise that responsibility ranked but seventeenth on our list of lessons that children should learn through children's sports.

As one listens to the news, or reads a magazine or newspaper, it seems that fewer and fewer people are willing to accept responsibility for their own actions. The headline read *Fog Responsible for Ten-car Pileup*. This conjures an image of a giant hand made out of fog reaching out and pushing cars into one another. A responsible person adjusts to inclement weather conditions, or simply stays at home. It's about choice and ensuing consequences. Whether or not you chose to drive in the fog is a decision that rests entirely with you, and, although there may be outside forces influencing your decision, you must bear the responsibility of your choice.

We all make hundreds of decisions every day, the consequences of which depend on circumstances. Our actions are based on our own experiences and motivations, and it's important that children learn that each decision bears a consequence.

You may recall a few years ago, the media reported on the tragic story of a seven-year-old girl who attempted to fly across the United States and back, accompanied by her father and her flight instructor. We heard, read or listened to the telling and retelling of a gifted child who had learned to fly a light aircraft. She was attempting to set a flying record, which, were she successful, would have brought her fame and financial reward, likely through product endorsement. We accept the story at face value that while attempting to take off in inclement weather, they crashed. She tried, she failed, she died. Many of us cried for that precocious little girl, and view her premature death as one of life's tragedies.

But there is much this story misses. Some questioned risking the life of a child for a record, and others wondered why children are allowed to fly airplanes. Psychologist Allan Goebel wrote an analysis of the incident with regard to responsibility, which appeared in a local newspaper. In it he asked some uncomfortable questions and drew some nasty conclusions, echoing the feelings of many of us who followed the story.

> *"Jessica Dubroff, seven, is dead, along with her father and flight instructor. Jessica's mother is quoted as saying that she would want all her children to 'die in a state of joy'. I suspect that although Jessica loved flying and wanted to fly until she died, she likely died in a state of fear and confusion. She may have died wondering what had gone wrong, and wondering why the adults with her weren't protecting her or making things better.*
>
> *In what I read about Jessica's death, I don't recall any emphasis on responsibility, protecting children from harm and taking only calculated risks.*

What was so important to them that required them to have Jessica take off in conditions that would have tested the skill of an adult, veteran pilot?

Was her flying instructor trying to promote himself while allowing Jessica to take off under dangerous conditions? Was her father trying to validate his beliefs about child-rearing or was he trying to bask in reflected glory while encouraging a seven-year-old child to set a meaningless record? Didn't Jessica's mother realize she was putting Jessica and others at risk by allowing Jessica to explore, experiment, be free and just live her life?

As a society we need laws that prevent parents and organizations from exploiting children by putting them into dangerous, record-setting situations.

As parents we need to monitor ourselves constantly to ensure we don't sacrifice our children to promote our own values and ideas.

We need to remember that training is progressive, long-term and systematic. We need to be patient enough to do this training."

It is not only possible but imperative to draw a parallel between this alleged exploitation of a child to that of the obsession to win in little league. One might argue that it is ludicrous to equate the death of a small child with that of the potential hurt and humiliation a child might endure from a determined coach or overzealous parents. I heartily disagree and further assert that the damage some children experience through little league is life-long and debilitating. Our letters have proven this.

A newborn child is utterly dependent on his or her parents. As children learn to walk and talk they begin the long journey to independence. Along the way they learn to judge for themselves and make their own decisions until, one day, the bird leaves the nest. But in the interim a child needs to be governed, and the task is not an easy one. Every parent knows how easy it is to allow a child to do as he wishes-to say "no!" incites confrontation and argument with the corollary being unwanted stress. Yet, there are times we simply must say no. Carol Burnett once said, "You've got to love your kids enough to let them hate you for a while."

Today's children are tomorrow's adults, yet there is increasing concern that we have lost control over a generation of young people. Are the children to blame or are they merely a product of their environment? An environment that we, the adults, have created? Do we accept responsibility for their errant attitudes?

Whatever your role in a child's life the reality is that we are all responsible for what children learn. Ultimately, parents bear the responsibility for the well-being of their children. Teachers have moral obligations to society and the children for what and how they teach each child.

Coaches are there for a variety of reasons. Some believe they have something to teach the children while others believe they are performing a community service. Others coach because they have a son or daughter on the team. There are likely as many reasons as there are coaches, yet one common thread binds all of these individuals-the responsibility to set the best possible example as a figure of authority in those children's lives, because your coaching could have life-long effects.

Gerry Crowley

Ryan, from Spokane, Washington, writes:

During spring and summer while growing up in the late fifties, I used to play baseball with the neighborhood kids. We played in back yards and vacant lots. We'd pretended we were Mickey Mantle, Sandy Koufax or Willie Mays, cheered by thousands of fans in the make-believe stadium.

During the eighth grade I looked forward to the coming baseball season. This would be my first opportunity to play on a real team. What a thrill it was to receive a T-shirt with my school name and a cap with the school colors and letter. I wasn't particularly strong or co-ordinated at that age, but I was there for every practice and tried my hardest. I don't recall the coach working with me to improve my skills and technique as he did with the other kids who had potential. I was there for every game, hoping for my chance to play.

Finally, the last game of the season came and I was there, hopeful, as ever, that I'd get to play. Each inning my heart would race, hoping and praying the coach would call my name. He never did. I don't recall if we won that final game. I can't recall if we even won any games. What I do remember is that I never got a chance to play.

My mom picked me up after that final game and I simply couldn't control the tears. That was the first time I told her that I hadn't played at all, the entire season.

I neither played nor attended a baseball game or any other sporting event for over twenty years.

If you still think your coaching isn't directly affecting the lives of the children on your team, please read Ryan's letter again. Individuals like Ryan have had value judgements made about them based on a coach's perception of their physical prowess. There is no greater folly!

In your hands you hold their well-being. You have that power. It's an awesome responsibility.

FOR PARENTS AND COACHES: RESPONSIBILITY

Are coaches and parents taking true responsibility for their own actions? Do they understand the relationship between the examples that they provide and the behavior of the charges? Is true responsibility on the part of the children rewarded?

XI: WHAT IT'S ALL ABOUT

Children that participate in any activity will remember something about it the rest of their lives. The best part is that while those memories are being created the experience, when put in proper perspective, can be fun for parents, coaches, and most importantly, the children.

Having Fun
Perspective

Having Fun – *6th precept*

> *"If those who are the enemies of innocent amusements
> had the direction of the world, they would take away
> the spring, and youth, the former from the year, the
> latter from human life." -Balzac*

This chapter is the most important because it talks about having fun, that wonderful medium through which all lessons can be learned. It is part of the natural make-up of all children to want to have fun, motivating them to read, paint, listen to music, watch a movie, and, yes, play a game. When guiding a child toward a certain goal, your aim must be to create enthusiasm, rather than anxiety, because an anxious child learns nothing.

Think back to when you were in school getting ready to write an exam, or read aloud in class, or run the two-hundred meter dash. Chances are you were nervous, which caused untold misery, physically and mentally. You simply cannot function optimally when the body is trembling; it feels like your muscles have turned to mush, and your thinking process seems to have shut down. A coach's bullying can cause all of these things in youngsters not experienced enough to turn nervous energy into performance. Encourage *effort*, not outcome.

This philosophy is stated poignantly by a teen-aged referee whose frustration caused her to write this letter to the editor.

> *"'Christopher!' A woman screeches. 'Christopher! Get a move on it!'*
>
> *'Christopher!' Another voice. 'Go for the ball!'*
>
> *Christopher's head swivels as he listens first to his mother, then to his soccer coach, unsure of whose instructions to follow. He knows he should listen to the coach, but dreads the ride home if he ignores the shrill voice of his parent. He decides to pretend he hasn't heard either of them, and kicks the ball out of bounds.*
>
> *The teenage referee calls a corner kick for the other team. Both mother and coach now shift their anger to the referee, who follows the boy's example and ignores them.*
>
> *It's not easy, for either the boy or the referee, to ignore the shouted insults and criticism from adult spectators. Referees, like me, mutter all the smart comebacks and crushing answers we can think of ... thoughts we know we can never say aloud, for to do so would be to reduce our authority and dignity to the level of the parent.*
>
> *For adult referees, it's an unpleasant, but routine, part of the job. But for youth referees the constant*

condemnation is unsettling and demoralizing, not to mention personally wounding.

I will always remember the time when, at 14, in my first year of refereeing, a coach yelled at me for five minutes for accidentally cutting two minutes off an unimportant game.

Then, there was the time when I was running lines and a parent stood just behind me, criticizing every call I made against his team, softly enough that only I could hear. When I called the center referee over to instruct this man to leave, he denied saying anything. Furthermore, the other spectators became angry when we insisted that he leave.

Officials of children's sports, whether referees or umpires, are people whose imperfections and minor mistakes are regularly met with abuse and insults that would be considered unacceptable in any other situation. I have been told to 'get glasses, stay home,' and asked, 'what's a girl doing on the field?' I have been called names and been sworn at.

The worst part is, you can't yell back. The parents are already setting a bad enough example for the kids. The referees, at least, have to be cool and professional. That's a lot to ask of an uncertain, insecure teenager.

Refereeing would be fun if it weren't for the adults. While there's the odd player who follows the example of the spectators and coaches, most of the kids are pleasant and co-operative. They will chat with you, tease you, and if you make a mistake they will let you know in a way that isn't personally insulting or rude. Many parents get overly involved *in kid's sports because they see themselves in their children. As one woman commented to Christopher's mother, 'We want to win more than they do!'*

I wonder if those belligerent, determined parents will still see themselves in their children when those children become belligerent, determined teenagers who defy authority and swear when they don't get their way."

Our behavior as adults-the example we are meant to set-and its direct effect on young, yet undeveloped, minds, is summed up eloquently in the last paragraph of this young referee's letter.

"I wonder if those belligerent, determined parents will still see themselves in their children when those children become belligerent, determined teenagers who defy authority and swear when they don't get their way."

Thoreau wrote, "It takes two to speak the truth - one to speak, and another to hear." Are we listening?

Recently, a friend of mine recounted this experience from her own son's life, by way of support of the philosophies contained in this book.

"When George was in elementary school, each day he would come home and get on the telephone to 'round up the guys' for a game of scrub, or whatever other sport they decided to play that day. I was often amazed at how much discussion went on over specific points within the rules - rules that they would bend

at liberty based on how many came out to play and the caliber of play for the day.

Occasionally, events erupted into an argument, but I found that, by and large, left on their own, they would play happily for hours, day after day after day. They must have been having fun or they wouldn't have carried on. In fact, I loved it when they played street hockey right outside my house because they laughed and cheered endlessly. They sounded like children are supposed to sound.

When George would finally come in after these pick-up games, he was always in a great mood, bubbling on and on to me about every last detail of the game. If I would ask which team won he would look at me curiously, as if I had asked a really stupid question. Why? Because it didn't matter. What counted to these kids was their own performance as it related to a particular assist, save, shot, and so on.

George is now almost seventeen-years-old and he and his friends still play pick-up. The sport still varies, the rules still vary, yet what is unchanged is their delight."

Why, then, is winning so important to adults? That is not a simple question and the answer is equally complicated. Average parents will probably tell you that they want their child to be successful and that means winning. A coach might feel that there's no point putting a team together if it isn't going to win. By now you should see that these answers lack perspective. They have little to do with the needs of children and more to do with egos of adults. Sports psychologist, Dr. Eric Margenau, believes that the explanation lies in the insecurities of adults. He states:

> *The key element for parents to recognize is that a parent's desires can be, and often are, a function of his or her own lack of self-esteem and need to live vicariously and experience excellence through the performance of the child.*
>
> *The parent who feels secure, competent, and adequate in the world isn't going to do that to a child."*

In the surveys that I conducted, when I asked what children should be learning, the number-one response was sportsmanship. Having fun was number six. Yet, when children up to age 15 were asked the same question, their number-one response was having fun! Why is that? Is it reasonable to consider that children really don't care about winning as long as they have fun? Is it possible to learn from the children?

We take a game-a diversion for amusement-we organize it, we add rules, we change rules, we bring in coaches, we bring in arbiters, we keep track of the score. But do we make it better?! The fact of the matter is that when we involve ourselves in the play of children, we don't always make things better.

If you want to coach children in a meaningful way that will have a positive impact on their lives, then you must remember to maintain a proper perspective. Put as much fun into your coaching as you possibly can. It's the fun the children will remember long after the score is forgotten.

FOR PARENTS AND COACHES: HAVING FUN

Consider whether rewards or negative reinforcements are being used regularly with the children. What kinds of negative reinforcement are being tolerated? Should they be? What kinds of rewards are provided to the children? Are the children taught to seek for nothing but the abstract gleam of a trophy off in the distance-with nothing for the teams that don't "win" at the end of the season or tournament? Or are children taught to enjoy their own development, their own accomplishments, their team advances in combining skills as the season goes along, and rewarded for that hard work and for trying their best? Is time for fun built into practices?

Perspective – *20th precept*

> *"For some must follow, and some must command though all are made of clay!" -Longfellow*

> *"From the error of others, a wise man corrects his own." -Syrus*

How important is the outcome of a kid's game compared with the lessons and the memories that each child will take away from being a participant? Children need to be spoken to in a positive manner and with positive encouragement.

Will your coaching style be the turning point in some child's life that builds self-esteem, confidence and character, or will you be the reason he never reaches full potential?

It is uncanny how children remember moments from their past as though these were locked in time. As a coach you have the power to build a child up or knock him down.

Throughout this guide, you have probably caught glimpses of yourself in the words. If nothing else, I hope I have shown that your influence on the children you coach is direct and commanding. That means the responsibility you have undertaken is really quite awesome. Remember that children who sign up to play little league sports just want to have fun, especially when they are young, and that is what your focus must be. You must put that into an overall perspective of character development for each young life that you touch. Chances are, when dealing with children, if there is a problem, your focus is on winning and you have lost true perspective.

If there is even a little of Coach Eddie in the way you coach, it is time to change. You need to put things in proper perspective. After all, even Coach Eddie was able to change, and if he can change, so can you. How do I know that Coach Eddie has changed?

Coach Eddie wrote this book.

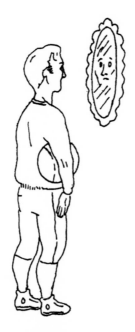

Don't judge him too harshly lest you recognize him in the mirror...

Gerry Crowley

FOR PARENTS AND COACHES: PERSPECTIVE

Are teams managed and led as if they were adult professional teams? Do coaches expect obedient little machines in their players, or are their relationships human and encouraging? Are the children happy when they practice, happy when they play, and happy after games, regardless of whether or not they won?

XII: CONCLUSION

"Children have more need of models than of critics."
-Joubert

It seems so very long ago that I first asked that all-important question that led to this book. I asked: "What should coaches be teaching children?" A simple question that produced hundreds of not-so-simple replies.

It has been said that to be the best you can be you must combine skill with a positive attitude. When I asked seminar participants, coaches, and parents to define whether each precept referred to a skill or an attitude, the overwhelming response favored attitude. This holds true in sports as well as in life. The message is very clear. Eighty-five percent of what you teach children should be about the right attitude.

A coaches job, albeit voluntary, goes far beyond passing on athletic skills. You must be part psychologist, part philosopher, part confidant, part teacher-the complete role model. Tough gig, isn't it?

Not at all, if you maintain the right attitude. Maybe you thought showing up and winning were enough. Not only are they non-starters, they demonstrate a philosophy that can be detrimental to the development of a child.

There will always be children who possess exceptional skills with major league potential. Exceptional skill will never be the reason for failure to make it to the major leagues, but a bad attitude could very easily lead to failure. When you coach children you become an authority figure in their lives as well as a role model. The decisions you make may very well have a life-long effect on each one of those children. You must consider whether those decisions will create a fond memory for the child, or will those decisions be the reason the child never participates again?

There is far more at stake than winning the game where children are involved.

The game is over. We lost. But the little leaguers are smiling and munching pizza. Those smiles are your reward. They tell you that the children are happy. Their smiles are proof that there is such a thing as...

...winning without winning!

FOR PARENTS AND COACHES: CONCLUSION

If you have carefully followed your list of what coaches should be teaching throughout this book and made notes about your own organization's good and not-so-good aspects, you will already have a much clearer idea of where work needs to be done. It's a good idea to prioritize this list, and begin the slow process of altering the organization from within, and by *your own example*. Sometimes elements of improvement can be made simply by talking to a fellow coach or to your child's coach. Sometimes what will be needed is a set of organizational objectives that can be provided to all the coaches and parents as models for improvement in various areas.

Keep in mind that blaming and anger are not the answers. Coaches are human, too. Sometimes coaches flounder because of inadequate training or a lack of direction about what parents and children's sports organizations want them to teach. Support, instruction and consultation are very important for coaches as well.

Working on attitude, on one important element at a time, and deeply understanding the responsibilities of coaches and parents in kid's sports over time can transform an organization and make it a truly wonderful and fulfilling place for the children involved in it.

ABOUT THE AUTHOR

Gerry Crowley, children's sports consultant and coach, has spent many years working with kids, coaches and parents in seminars and in coaching, as well as at the organizational level, to develop positive environments for children. Crowley spent more than 6 years researching and writing this book. He is the father of two boys and has 3 grandchildren.